RELEVANCE OF SWAMI VIVEKANANDA IN 21ST CENTURY

RELEVANCE OF SWAMI VIVEKANANDA IN 21ST CENTURY

Sunita Mangla
Asst. Professor Kalindi College,
Delhi University

KALPAZ

ISBN : 978-93-5128-018-7

Price : ₹ 630

First Published 2014

Published by

Kalpaz Publications
C-30, Satyawati Nagar,
Delhi-110052
Ph. : 9212142040
E-mail: kalpaz@hotmail.com

Laser Typesetting : Rudra Computer Graphics, Delhi
Printed at : G. Print Process, Delhi

Cataloging in Publication Data—DK
Courtesy: D.K. Agencies (P) Ltd. <docinfo@dkagencies.com>

Relevance of Swami Vivekananda / Sunita.
p. cm.
Contributed articles.
Includes bibliographical references and index.
ISBN 9789351280187

1. Vivekananda, Swami, 1863-1902—Political and social views. 2. Education—India—Philosophy. I. Sunita (Assistant professor of political science)

DDC 181.4 23

Dedicated to
My Father
"Sh. Shersingh Mangla"

Contents

Preface

Swami Vivekananda holds a pride of place among the makers of modern India. He was one of the greatest patriots to have ever been born in this country. During his visit to Belur Math, Mahatma Gandhi said, "I have gone through his works very thoroughly and after having gone through them, the love that I have for my country became a thousand fold." Jawaharlal Nehru said, "Directly or indirectly he has powerfully influenced the modern India of today and I think that our younger generation will take advantage of this fountain of wisdom, of spirit and fire that flows through Swami Vivekananda". Shri Rabindranath Tagore said, "If you want to know India, study Vivekananda. In him everything is positive and nothing negative." A large number of his friends and admirers repeatedly spoke about his love and passion for mother India.

The 150th birthday of Swami Vivekananda was celebrated all over India and in different countries of the world. Ministry of Youth Affairs and Sports of India decided to observe 2013 as the year of 150th Birth Anniversary of Swami Vivekananda. The present book "The Relevance of Swami Vivekananda in 21st Century" is the fitting tribute to the icon of modern India on his 150th Birth anniversary.

The First chapter contributed by Dr. Anula Maurya comprehensively deals with the various facets of thoughts of

Swami Vivekananda and his concept of ideal society. The ideas of Swami Vivekananda are still relevant today and act like the torchbearer for the modern generation.

The Second chapter written by Mr. Sheshadri Chari deals with vision of Swami Vivekananda and its relevancy to the modern India. He talks about the relevancy of thoughts of Swami Vivekananda in shaping conscience of modern India.

The Third chapter contributed by the editor of the book Dr. Sunita Mangla talks about relevance of Vivekananda in the modern age and how his thoughts are everlasting. Millions of youths world over treat Vivekananda as their ideal and spiritual Guru. The message of Vivekananda is not limited to only India but for the whole humanity.

The Fourth chapter of the book is written by Dr. Naved Jamal who deals with importance of Vivekananda in the modern times. Vivekananda's address to the parliament of world religions has set a new course of history in the life of Vivekananda.

The Fifth chapter written by Dr. Deepak Yadav talks about role of Vivekanada's philosophy in shaping the lives of millions of youths worldover. The philosophy of Vedanta which consists gist of his thoughts has a great significance today.

Sixth chapter of the book is contributed by Dr. Deepak Yadav who tries to convey the message of Vivekananda who is the ideal of millions of youths world over. Vivekananda awakened pride of millions of downtrodden whom he treated as Daridranarayan and he blamed greedy rich people behind their apathy.

The Seventh chapter of the book is written by Dr. Nivedita Giri talks about political ideas of Swami Vivekananda and its relevancy today. At the time when corruption and immorality has taken over the noble profession of politics in India, the life of Vivekananda is itself is the message for our leaders today.

The Eighth chapter of the book contributed by Dr. V. Shirisha deals with Vivekananda's views on education. Vivekananda treated education as a revolutionary medium to change the fate of humanity.

The Ninth chapter of the book written by Ms. Niharika deals with relevance of thoughts of Swami Vivekananda on education in 21st century. Education is the most powerful weapon in the hands of weaker sections of society.

The last chapter of the book written by Dr. Seema Mathur talks about Vivekananda's views on Hindu religion. Hindu religion always believed in sarvdharmasamabhava.

My sincere thanks to all my colleagues and friends who have given articles for this book. Special thanks goes to Dr. Sanghmittra (deputy director in Indian Council for Historical Research) for valuable help and encouragement and providing financial support for organising seminar on this topic. I am also thankful to Dr. Anula Maurya (principal, Kalindi College) who inspired me to write this book. I am also thankful to Prof. M.P. Singh, Prof. Veena Kukreja, all contributors specially Dr. Deepak Yadav, scholars, family members and above all to dear students who have always been the inspiration for me behind this endeavour.

Finally I owe special thanks to Mr. Sheshdri Chari (Executive Director, Forum for Strategic and Security Studies, New Delhi) for the personal interest he took in getting this book out of the press with promptness and efficiency and have benefitted from the suggestions made by my contributors while editing this book. The entire responsibility, however, of the form in which it has been presented is mine and therefore for shortcomings I alone be blamed.

Sunita Mangla

List of Contributors

Nivedita Giri, Assistant Professor, Department of Political Science, Kalindi College.

Sunita Mangla, Assistant Professor, Department of Political Science, Kalindi College, University of Delhi.

V. Shirisha, Assistant Professor, Kalindi College, University of Delhi.

Niharika Tiwari, Assistant Professor, Department of Political Science, Kalindi College, University of Delhi.

Seema Mathur, Assistant Professor, Department of Political Science, Kalindi College, University of Delhi.

Anula Maurya, Principal, Kalindi College, University of Delhi.

Deepak Yadav, Assistant Professor, Department of Political Science, Kalindi College, University of Delhi.

Naved Jamal, Assistant Professor, Department of Political Science, Jamia Millia Islamia, Delhi.

Deepak Yadav, Assistant Professor, Department of Political Science, Kalindi College, University of Delhi.

Sheshadri Chari, Executive Director, Forum for Strategic and Security Studies, New Delhi, India.

1

Swami Vivekananda: His Concept of Ideal Society

Anula Maurya

"Where should you go to seek for God? Are not all the poor; the miserable, the weak Gods? Why not worship them first? Why to dig a well on the shores of the Ganga? Let the poor people your God think of them, work for them, and pray for them incessantly - the Lord will show you the way".

Swami Vivekananda

Swami Vivekananda (1863-1902) was a mystic personality. Although of athletic muscular build, he had a deep consciousness like Platonism and Spinoza attend with the absolute elastic principles. But at the sametime, he was a great intellectual at home in the resets of metaphysical Vedantism, European philosophy and the elements of modern science and had a burning enthusiasm for the alleviation of the human suffering especially for the poor people.

Swami Vivekananda believed untouchability as the most heinous crime against humanity. He vehemently criticised those Hindus who justified untouchability in the name of Hindu tradition which is being practiced for centuries. According to him—The Indian Civilisation since ages has been afflicted by social evils. He felt that social reform through religion could not be possible without bringing spiritual reform first.

Swami Vivekananda believed that he could not preach even religion to Americans without showing them its practical effect on social life. He could not go to England without showing the wonderful political changes the Vedanta would bring. So in India, soul reform had to be preached by showings how much it would improve the one thing that the nation wanted, its spirituality.[1]

Swami Vivekananda on Women

Swami Vivekananda was the champion of an anticipation of women and believed in complete equality. According to him, in modern Hinduism which is largely Puranik i.e., post-Buddhistic in origin, the status of women became somewhat inferior. But certainly, the Aryan ideal of womanhood was distinctly higher. He wanted women to be self dependent economically, socially and culturally so that they can take decisions for themselves independently.

Vivekananada cited the examples of **Apalla, Gargi, Ghosa, Lopamudra** were some of the prominent women scholars who wrote the hymns of *Rigveda* and were equally learned in Hindu philosophy like other Hindu male saints. He said that women participated in *Yagnas* and sacrificial practices.

Swami Vivekananda vehemently opposed the child marriage. He cited many examples from Vedas and Puranas which prohibits the marriage at the tender age. Women should be given freedom to choose their own life partner. Proper training should be given to them so that they could learn about the importance of renunciation and this would certainly help them in practicing virginity thought their life. Apart from this, they should be taught sciences and other things which would be beneficial not only to them but also to the society at large.

According to Vivekananda, only through education we will be able to eradicate century old social evils against women and downtrodden sections of society. Women should be given education because if a woman gets education, she will make the whole family educated and in return we will have a better society.

Swami Vivekananda was the champion of community life and he emphasised that true freedom can only be realised in a community life. Western concept of individuality will lead to loneliness and towards an atomised society.

Swami Vivekananda on Freedom

Vivekananda goes on to add that man was born free (like *Rousseau*) but life constrained his natural freedom making him an atomised, isolated, lovely individual who was solely interested in the unrestrained pursuit of his desires and aims which would sooner or later brings him into conflict with equalent freedom of another, thus cancelling each other out. He was against the self-centered salvation. According to Vivekananda:

"If you seek your own salvation, you will go to hell. It is the salvation of others that you must seek; and even if you have to go to hell in working for others that is worth more than to gain heaven by seeking your own salvation."[2]

While the qualities of individuality were essential for the development of his full personality and his creative potentialities, but equally is important in his social nature and his spiritual self. According to Swami Vivekananda, it was possible for both individuality and sociality to go together so that where man's individual self was restrained by his built in sociality, it would provoke resistance from the others the same kinds of individuals.

According to Swamiji, freedom is natural to the human beings so the restraints on freedom will also have to come from natural order to retain its spontaneity. Hence, such constraints on freedom will have to come from religion since it alone could develop in human beings, the relationship between individuality and sociality and raise it to sufficiently higher order of spiritual consciousness. Vivekananda felt that certain circumstances compelled men to act in a way which restrained the freedom of others as well as went against his own will. This could not amount to realisation of a true freedom. Therefore, the purpose of limiting men's freedom should be for the better and refined quality of freedom and not repression.

Swami Vivekananda always emphasised on belief in us. According to him:

"*If you have faith in the three hundred and thirty millions of your mythological Gods, and in all Gods which foreigners have introduced into your midst, and still have no faith in yourselves, there is no salvation for you. Have faith in yourselves and stand up on that faith.*"[4]

Swami Vivekananda further elaborates that:

"*The history of the world is the history of a few men who had faith in themselves. That faith calls out the Divinity within. You can do anything. You fail when you do not strive sufficiently to manifest infinite power. As soon as man or a nation loses faith in himself or itself, death comes. Belief first in yourself and then in God.*"

Swami Vivekananda on Caste

Swami Vivekananda was ferociously against the caste and argued that caste oppression has nothing to do with the religion and it could very easily be destroyed without causing any harm to Hinduism. According to him form Buddha to Rammohan Roy, every one committed the mistake of holding caste to be a religious institution and tried to pull down religion and caste together and failed miserably.

Swami Vivekananda was inspired by the ideal of social harmony and synthesis embodied in the theory of Varna system of ancient India. He therefore earnestly wanted that the caste system must be ennobled. The basic point is not to impose a system of dull uniformity on society but to help everybody in attaining the status of a true Brahman. He however densoured priestraft in vigorous terms because it penetrated social tyranny and disregarded masses.[5]

In 1893, he wrote notwithstanding the low claims of priests, caste was simply a crystallised social institution which after doing its service filled the atmosphere of India with its stench and it could only be removed by giving back to the people their lost social individuality. Every man who was born here knew that he was a man. Every man born in India knew that he was a slave of the society. With the introduction of modern competition, caste was disappearing fast. No religion was necessary to kill it.[6]

He condemned the old Orthodox Brahminical doctrine of Adhikanand. This doctrine propounds the exclusion of the Shudras or the rest of the masses from the benefit of the Vedic knowledge. Sankara also adhered to this undemocratic dogma. But Vivekananda heroically championed the concept of spiritual equality. He stated that all men are equal and equally entitled to spiritual wisdom and gnosis of the highest type, this democratic spiritualism was indeed a radical step. Even the Upanishads sanction some kind of Adhikaswad which is a plea for spiritual aristocracy. But Vivekananda wanted that the highest truth should be broadest without any compromise. He said – "Thus you will confer the greatest blessing on the masses, unshackle their bondages and uplift the whole nation".[7]

According to Vivekananda, the fourfold differentiation of the social order also represent an ideal type, but he rebelled against the oppressions and repressions practiced by the so called upper castes and stated that—"But that does not mean that those should be these privileges. They should be knocked on the head."[8] It is true that however deeply concerned about functional differential one may be, a Varna system is bound to have undesirable social effects. We find that about the 10th century BC, Brahmanas developed on elaborate religious and spiritual cult to strengthen their social superiority which was attacked by Buddha. Once more, twenty five hundred years afterwards, Swami Vivekananda had called the Bhahmanas of Madras "Pariahs of Pariahs" when letter had the effrontery to say that Vivekananda as a non-Brahmana had no right to adopt the Sanyasi's Garb.[9]

According to him, Caste has become an oppressing institution which is an perverted form of Varna system. For the stagnant life of Indian masses, he blamed the priests and land-lords which saddened him heart. He treated these classes like leaches who are sucking the blood of Indian masses and enjoying the life of plenty, whereas millions are dying of hunger and starvation.

The caste system, which had originally been devised to emphasise the organic unity of Hindu Society, was now petrified. Its real purpose had seem to protect the weak from the ruthless competition of the strong and to indicate the supremacy of spiritual knowledge over the power of military weapons, wealth and organised labour, but now it was sapping the vitality of the masses.

Swami Vivekananda claimed that right to priesthood should not be decided by birth but by knowledge. Anybody from four Varnas can become Brahmana if he is well-versed in Vedas and Shastras. He said that due to monopoly of Brahmanas on the Hindu religions scriptures they have made Hindu religion as the kitchen religion. He blamed the priestly class being the frog of the well has damaged the Hindu society much more than the Christian Missionaries. Our religion has become like "do not touch me, I am seared".[10]

According to Vivekananda, Indian masses are the victims of the unscrupulous whims of their rulers, landlords, and priests. The tyranny of caste had sucked their last drop of blood. In most of the so called leaders, who shouted from the housetops for the liberation of the people, he had seen selfishness personified. He gave the call to the modern India to break down the barriers of caste, colour, and creed and fuse all people in to one humanity.

According to Vivekananda, it is difficult to destroy historical traditions so long as the four terms of Vedic Sociology - *Brahmanas, Kshetriyas, Vaishyas* and *Shudras* are retained, they are bound to perpetuate painful historical memories of social exploitation and suppression. He believed that a profound revolution is the need of India. The worst feature of caste is that it suppresses competition and the checking of competition has really been the cause of the political downfall of India and its conquest by foreign races.

Vivekananda on Religion

Swami Vivekananda believed that essence of Hinduism lies in the Gita, the Upanishads and the Sutras. The term 'Vedanta' covers various visions of thoughts propounded by Sankara, Ramanujam, Madhava, Chaitanya and Others. It includes Advaita, Visistha - dvaita and the dualist system of thought. Vivekananda said that there was no incompatibility among these different systems of thought. The human mind began with dualism, rose to qualified dualism and ultimately reached to qualified monism or Advaita which proclaimed the highest truth: Tat Twam Asi (Thou Art That). To him, Vedanta made an attempt to find out the ultimate unity of things.[11]

Vivekananda strongly criticised all kinds of orthodoxy in the matters of religion as they were nothing but, "Kitchen religion and don't touchism". While condemning the imposition of Western values and religion on India he argued that India was not only mother of spiritualism but also spread the message of peace throughout the world. The concept of *Vasudhaivkutumbakam* (whole earth is a family) given by Hinduism is the testimony that Hinduism is spreading the voice of love and harmony on earth since the time immemorial.

Vivekananda strongly condemned social evils, social exclusiveness, caste hierarchy untouchability, etc., which is being practiced in India in the name of religion. He said that no religion in the world does a step motherly treatment to its own people the manner in which Hinduism is doing. He called upon the complete eradication of untouchability from Hinduism and championed the cause of equal rights to all the citizens.

Vivekananda further argued that the essence of religion was love, service, sacrifice and remuneration and it inculcated in to the minds of people virtues like courage, brevity, purity, passion, love sympathy etc. Only material progress of nation can never make it proud unless spiritual upliftment is not attached with this.

Vivekananda believed that Hinduism had been subject of intense misrepresentation at the hands of Christian missionaries who suffered from imperialism complex and were actuated with a sense of burden to 'civilise' the black men and brown men by clearing the road for economic exploitation of Asia and Africa. But Hinduism to Vivekananda, a comprehensive gospel which could shelter within its blossom the profound philosophic intellect by its Nyaya, Samkhya and Vedanta.

To Vivekananda, Hinduism is the mother of religions and this can be to some extent demonstrated historically. Four major religions - Hinduism, Buddhism, Sikhism, and Jainism have taken birth in the holy land of India. The older Vedic religion also influenced the religion of Persia and Media and the reformist ethical movement which began in Judah in 6th century BC was inspired by some aspects of western Asiatic religions (Persia and India) which the Jews came to learn during the Babylonish captivity.[12]

European critics level the charges against the idealistic and illusionistic schools of Indian philosophy of being indifferent to ethics. Dr. A. B. Kieth has boldly said that, "in comparison with the intellectual activity of the Brahmanas, the ethical content of the Upanishads must be said to be negligible and valueless, they have completely failed to see that morality is the most objective and essential part of philosophy."[13]

According to Vivekananda, the universe was an illusory expression of the Brahma, the creator. *Maya* or *illusion* contained virtues such as knowledge, creativity and instinctive desires which infact was the visible image of the creator. Brahma has the immense responsibility to hold the universe together and its influence was felt in each and every object of his creation. The difference between Brahma and his creation was the finitude of virtues in its material forms. Each person had a different combination of unequal development of virtues. Every person with his dominant virtue therefore formed a part of the larger whole. Hence, the goal of individual can only be find its true expression in the entire humanity. Vivekananda called the attaining of the 'Brahmaners' by man, the state of '**Moksha**'.[14]

In The Parliament of World Religions

On Monday, September 11, 1893, the first session of the Parliament was opened in the great Hall of Columbus, where were seated representatives of the religious beliefs of twelve hundred millions of human race. In the center sat Cardinal Gibbons, the highest prelate of the Roman Catholic Church on the western continent. On the right and left of him were gathered the Oriental delegates - Pratap Chandra Majumdar of Bengal and Nagarkar of Bombay who were representatives of the Brahmo Samaj. Other prominent figure from India included Annie Besant, and Mr. Chakravarti from Bengal.

At length, in the late afternoon when the Chairman insisted, the Swami rose and bowed down to **Saraswati**–the Goddess of learning. His face glories like fire. His eyes surveyed in a swap the huge assembly before him. When he opened his lips, his spunch was like a torque of flame. It was the first time that he had to speak before such a august assembly and as the delegates, presented one by one, the Swami let his turn go by hour after hour until the end of the day.

When, Vivekananda's term came hardly he announced the opening words - "***Sisters and Brothers of America***", When hundreds rose to their feet with deferring shouts of applause. The Parliament had gone mad-everyone cheering Swamiji enthusiastically. For the two minutes he attempted to speak, but the words of wild enthusiasm created by this significant form of address prevented him. He was certainly the first to cast off the formalism of the Congress and speak to the audience in the language for which they were waiting when silence was restored, Swami greeted the youngest of the nations in the name of the most ancient order of monks in the world—The Vedic order of Sanyasins - and presented Hinduism as the mother of all religions. As religion which has taught the world both tolerance and universal acceptance. He quoted two beautiful, illustrative passages taken from the scriptures of Hinduism.

"*As the different streams having their sources in different places, all mingle their water in the sea, O Lord, the different paths which men take taught difference tendency, various though they may appear created or straight, all lied to thee*".

"*Whoseover comes to me, through whatsoever form, I reach him, all men are struggling through paths which in the end will leap to Me.*"

It was only a short speech but its spirit of universality, its fundamental earnestness and broadmindedness completely captivated the whole assembly. There were other Hindu delegates who stood for societies or churches or sects but the Swami, who belonged to seat but rather to India as a whole, proclaimed the universality of religious truths and sameness of the God of all religious realisations. In the course of this illuminating address during the sessions of the Parliament, the Swami placed before the distinguished audience the cardinal truths of Vedanta, the Universal religion of humanity.

Swami Vivekananda, although speaking on behalf of Hinduism did not speak narrowly for his one religion only, but gave the message of peace and brotherhood and called for establishing a harmonal relationship among all religions of the world. He further elaborated by saying that God is like the Ocean in which many rivers mingles and lose their identity. Therefore, like this there are many religions in the world like the rivers but ultimately they reach to one God who is supreme. Paths may be different but the destiny is the same.

Conclusion

Swami Vivekananda was one of the few jewels in the crown of Hinduism who showed the path of virtuousness and universal brotherhood and broadly interpreted the Hindu scriptures. He did not shy to attack the orthodox character of Hinduism which was justifying age old outdated practices like untouchability and caste system in the name of religion. He said if there is ever to be a universal religion, it must be one which will have no location in place or time, which will be infinite, like the God it will preach, and whose sun will shine upon the followers of Krishna and Christ, on saint and sinners alike; which will not be Brahminic or Buddhistic, Christian or Mohammedan but the sum total of all these, and still have infinite space of development, which in its Catholicity will find. Place for every human being from the lowest groveling savage not for removed from the brute to the highest man towering by the virtues of his hard heart almost above humanity.

References

1. Padhy, K.S. (2011)- *Indian Political Though;* New Delhi, PHI Learning Private Limited, pp. 95–114.
2. *The life of Vivekananda,* Vol. I, pp. 270–275.
3. Tejsavananda Swami (1995), "*A Short Life of Swami Vivekananda*" Kolkata Advaita Ashram Publication, pp. 106–110.
4. *The Complete Work of Swami Vivekananda*, Vol. II, p. 170.
5. Ibid., p. 353.
6. Padhy. op. cit, p. 111.
7. Verma, V.P., (2012) – "*Modern Indian Political Thought*". Agra Laxmi Narayan Agarwal Publication, p. 113.
8. Vivekananda, Swami (1996) "*On India and Her Problems*" Advaita Ashram Publication, Almora, pp. 77–80.
9. Verma op. cit, pp. 113-115.
10. *Complete work of Vivekananda, Vol. III*, pp. 170–195.

11. Padhy, op. cit, pp. 95-118.
12. Kieth, A.B., (1936); *Indian Historical Quarterly,* p. 573.
13. *Ibid.* pp. 573–574.
14. Pantham, T., and Deutsch K.N., "*Political Thought in Modern India*", 1986, Sage, New Delhi, pp. 142–148.

2

Rebuilding India on Swami Vivekananda's Vision

Sheshadri Chari

India has a long and unique history of superior performance, highest achievement and evolved systems. As a result she remained a pioneer and leader in the world. In the course of time, the nation had to face frequent invasions and attacks from outside. Subsequently different parts of India came under the domination of the alien forces for nearly one thousand years. The nation had to endure untold sufferings.

Maharishi Aurobindo notes: "This great and ancient nation was once the fountain of human life, the apex of human civilization, the exemplar of courage and humanity, the perfection of good government and settled society, the mother of all religions, the teacher of all wisdom and philosophy. It has suffered much at the hands of inferior civilizations and more savage peoples; it has gone down into the shadow of night and tasted often of the bitterness of death. Its pride has been trampled into the dust and its glory has departed. Hunger and misery and despair have become the masters of this fair soil, these noble hills, these ancient rivers, these cities whose life story goes back into pre-historic night."

The time tested native systems were subject to contempt and destruction during the alien rule. Foreign ideas and systems were thrust from above. With the result, the alien thoughts and practices began to occupy the central place in Indian life. Ultimately India had to lose much of her original approaches.

Great souls were aware of the consequences and advocated the need for a shift towards Indian approaches, long before independence. Swami Vivekananda underlined: "We must grow according to our nature. Vain is it to attempt the lines of action that foreign societies have engrafted upon us.... I do not condemn the institutions of other races; they are good for them, but not for us. This is the first lesson to learn. With other sciences, other institutions, and other traditions behind them, they have got their present system, We, with our traditions, with thousands years of Karma behind us, naturally can only follow our own bent, run in our grooves; and that we shall have to."

Aurobindo echoed similarly in 1909: "We have sought to regain life by following the law of another being than our own. We must return and seek the sources of life and strengthen within ourselves." But in spite of these sane warnings, changes in the required direction were not initiated after India became independent. The ruling classes continued to make India depend on the alien ideas and approaches.

This attitude pained the concerned citizens and prompted them to voice their opinions. The concerned citizens and prompted them to voice their opinions. The noted Gandhian Dharampal wrote: "Today, we feel encircled by hostility—much of it in fact generated by our own ineptitude and actions. From around 1947, we have treated ourselves as cousins of the West. Dominated by the West, it may be necessary at the moment to rely on Western knowledge and products. But this can be only be a short-term proposal."

But unfortunately the reliance on western ideas still continues even after sixty five years of independence. We remain unaware of our past as well as the present, and fail to pose the fundamental questions that are critical to us. To quote Dharampal: "Since Independence in 1947, it is this question of reconstruction of self and society on the foundation of our priorities, values, tradition and culture that seems to have completely eluded us, particularly our scholars, administrators and politicians. We appear to have forgotten that we can look back and learn from our own past, and based on that experience, construct our own unique identity within the context of our own affairs as well as that of the rest of the world. What do we as a nation—without learning on others' ideological and material crutches—want? Do we have ingenuity or not? Can we make our own points—as against aligning with one sort or another? Do we have a point to make as Indians?"

Times are changing fast. India is fast emerging as a powerful nation at the international level. The Indian thoughts, approaches and systems are getting increasingly recognized. Meanwhile, the west is facing serious difficulties at the economic, social and personal levels. The world is beginning to realize the unsuitability of the western models for other countries. No nation can make real progress on imported ideas.

It is time for us to understand that a strong India can be built only on the Indian foundations. The contemporary events reaffirm that India is fully capable of achieving a lot, provided serious efforts are made in the required direction. For this purpose, it is necessary to understand India - her past and present -from true perspectives. Misconceptions about the country have to be removed and correct opinions have to be formed. Vivekananda says: "We all hear so much about degradation of India. There was a time when I also believed in it. But today standing on the vantage-ground of experience, with eyes cleared of obstructive predispositions and above all, of the highly-coloured pictures of other countries tone down their proper shade and light by actual contact, I confess, in all humility, that I was wrong. Thou blessed land of Aryas, thou West never degraded. Sceptres have been broken and thrown away, the ball of power has passed from hand to hand, but in India, courts and kings have always touched only a few; the vast mass of people, from the highest to the lowest, has been left to pursue its own its inevitable course, the current of national life flowing at times slow and half-conscious, at others, strong and awakened. I stand in awe before the unbroken procession of scores of shining centuries, with here and there a dim link in the chain, only to flare up with added brilliance in the next, and there she is walking with her own majestic steps – my motherland – to fulfil her glorious destiny, which no power on earth or in heaven can check – the regeneration of man the brute in to man the God the God."

India can be rebuilt, as she has the fundamentals and the potential. She has the background and capacity to reach higher levels and guide the destiny of the other nations. It is the external thoughts and approaches that are hindering her from realizing the full potential. She has many problems and difficulties. But they can be solved if we decide to tackle them from the correct perspectives. For this purpose, let us recall the words of Swami Vivekananda: "This national ship, my countrymen, my children—this national ship has been ferrying millions and millions of souls across the waters of life.... But today, perhaps through your own fault, this boat has become a little damaged, has sprung a leak; Is it fit that you stand up and pronounce malediction upon it, one that has done more work than any other thing in the world? If there are holes in this national ship, this society of ours, we are its children. Let us go and stop the holes."

References

1. Dharmapal quoted in Indian Science and Technology in the Eighteenth Century, Other India Press, Goa, 1983.
2. Sri Aurobindo, Out of the ruins of the West ... India's Rebirth, Mira Aditi, Mysore, 1997.
3. Swami Vivekananda, My India The India Eternal, Ramakrishna Mission Institute of Culture, Calcutta, 2000.

3

Relevance of Swami Vivekananda in 21st Century

Sunita Mangla

Early Life

Vivekananda was born as Narendranath in Calcutta, the capital of British India, on 12th January 1863 during the Makar Sankranti festival. He belonged to a traditional Bengali *Kayastha* (a caste of Hindus) family and was one of the nine siblings. Narendra's father Vishwanath Datta was an attorney of Calcutta High Court. Narendra's mother was a pious woman and a housewife. The progressive rational approach of his father and the religious temperament of his mother helped shape his thinking and personality. Young Narendranath was fascinated by the wandering ascetics and monks.

Narendra's meeting with Ramakrishna in November 1881 proved to be a turning point in Narendra's life. Narendra said about this first meeting that:

"Ramakrishna looked just like an ordinary man, with nothing remarkable about him. He used the most simple

language and I thought 'Can this man be a great teacher?' I crept near to him and asked him the question which I had been asking others all my life: 'Do you believe in God, Sir?' 'Yes', he replied. 'Can you prove it, Sir?' 'Yes'. 'How?' 'Because I see him just as I see you here, only in a much intenser sense.' That impressed me at once, I began to go to that man, day after day, and I actually saw that religion could be given. One touch, one glance, can change a whole life."[1]

Narendra studied the works of David Hume, Immanuel Kant, Johann Gottlieb Fichte, Baruch Spinoza, Georg W. F. Hegel, Arthur Schopenhauer, Auguste Comte, Herbert Spencer, John Stuart Mill, and Charles Darwin. Narendra became fascinated with the evolutionism of Herbert Spencer and had correspondence with him. He translated Spencer's book *Education* (1861) into Bengali. Alongside his study of Western philosophers, he was thoroughly acquainted with Indian Sanskrit scriptures and many Bengali works. Dr. William Hastie, principal of General Assembly's Institution, wrote, "Narendra is really a genius. I have travelled far and wide but I have never come across a lad of his talents and possibilities, even in German universities, among philosophical students." Some accounts regard Narendra as a *srutidhara*—a man with prodigious memory.[2]

In 1888, Vivekananda left the monastery as a *Parivrâjaka*—the Hindu religious life of a wandering monk, "without fixed abode, without ties, independent and strangers wherever they go." His sole possessions were a *kamandalu* (water pot), staff, and his two favourite books—*Bhagavad Gita* and *The Imitation of Christ*. Vivekananda travelled extensively in India for five years, visiting centers of learning, acquainting himself with the diverse religious traditions and different patterns of social life. He developed sympathy for the suffering and poverty of the masses and resolved to uplift the nation. Living mainly on *bhiksha* (alms), Vivekananda travelled on foot and railway tickets bought by his admirers whom he met during the travels. During these travels he made acquaintance and stayed with Indians from all walks of life and religions—scholars, *dewans*, rajas, Hindus, Muslims, Christians, *pariahs* (low caste workers) and government officials.

Philosophy of Swami Vivekananda

Vivekananda stressed on different aspects of religion, education, character building as well as social issues pertaining to India. Vivekananda was a Hindu monk from India who played significant role in introducing *Vedanta* to the Western world and also reviving and redefining certain aspect of the religion within India. Rabindranath Tagore commented about Swami Vivekananda and his teachings, "If you want to know India, study Vivekananda. In him everything is positive and nothing negative." Vivekananda realised a country's future depends on its people, so he mainly stressed on man, "man-making is my mission", that's how he described his teaching. Vivekananda put his real ideals in few words and that was: "*To preach unto mankind their divinity and how to make it manifest in every movement of life.*"

Vivekananda linked morality with the control of mind. He saw truth, purity and unselfishness as traits, which strengthened the mind. He advised his followers to be holy, unselfish and have *Shraddha* (faith). He supported practice of *Brahmacharya* (celibacy), and believed that such practice was the source of his physical and mental stamina, as well as eloquence. Vivekananda emphasised that success was an outcome of focused thought and action. In his lectures on Raja Yoga, he said, "Take up one idea. Make that one idea your life - think of it, dream of it, live on that idea. Let the brain, muscles, nerves, and every part of your body, be full of that idea, and just leave every other idea alone. This is the way to success that is way great spiritual giants are produced."[3]

Religion

Swami Vivekananda was a follower of *Vedanta*. To Swami Vivekananda religion was not only talk or doctrine or theory, to him religion was realisation, as he said, "it is being and becoming, not hearing or acknowledging; it is the whole soul becoming changed into what it believes." He also felt religion is the gist of all worship is to be pure and to do good to others. According to Swami Vivekananda, religion is the idea, which is raising the brute into man, and man unto God. He firmly said, despondency can not be religion. According to Vivekananda, an important teaching he received from Ramakrishna was that *Jiva is Shiva* (each individual is divinity itself). So he stressed on *Shiva Jnane Jiva Seva*, (to serve common people considering them as manifestation of God). According to Vivekananda, man is potentially divine, so, service to man is indeed service to God.

Swami Vivekananda felt, the greatest misfortune of the world is we do not tolerate and accept other religions. In his lecture in Parliament of religions on September 15, 1893, he told a story of a frog who lived in a well for a long time. He was born there and brought up there and he used to think that nothing in the world can be bigger that. Swami Vivekananda concluded the story:—

"*I am a Hindu. I am sitting in my own little well and thinking that the whole world is my little well. The Christian sits in his little well and thinks the whole world is his well. The Mohammedan sits in his little well and thinks that is the whole world*".[4]

Parliament of the World's Religions opened on 11 September 1893 at the Art Institute of Chicago as part of the World's Columbian Exposition. On this day Vivekananda gave his first brief speech. He represented India and Hinduism. He was initially nervous, bowed to *Saraswati*, the Hindu goddess of learning and began his speech with, "Sisters and brothers of America!" To these words he got a standing ovation from a crowd of seven thousand, which lasted for two minutes. When silence was restored he began his address. He greeted the youngest of the nations on behalf of "the most ancient order of monks in the world, the Vedic order of Sannyasins, a religion which has taught the world both tolerance and universal acceptance." He quoted two illustrative passages from the *Shiva mahimnastotram*—"As the different streams having their sources in different places all mingle their water in the sea, so, O Lord, the different paths which men take, through different tendencies, various though they appear, crooked or straight, all lead to Thee!" and "Whosoever comes to me, through whatsoever form, I reach him; all men are struggling through paths that in the end lead to Me." Despite being a short speech, it voiced the spirit of the Parliament and its sense of universality.

Dr. Barrows, the president of the Parliament said, "India, the mother of religions was represented by Swami Vivekananda, the Orange-monk who exercised the most wonderful influence over his auditors." He attracted widespread attention in the press, which dubbed him as the "Cyclonic monk from India". The *New York Critique* wrote, "He is an orator by divine right, and his strong, intelligent face in its picturesque setting of yellow and orange was hardly less interesting than those earnest words, and the rich, rhythmical utterance he gave them." The *New York Herald* wrote, "Vivekananda is undoubtedly the greatest figure in the Parliament of Religions. After hearing him we feel how foolish it is to send missionaries to this learned nation." The American newspapers reported Vivekananda as "the greatest figure in the parliament of religions" and "the most popular and influential man in the parliament". The *Boston Evening Transcript* reported that Vivekananda was "a great favourite at the parliament…if he merely crosses the platform, he is applauded". He spoke several more times at the Parliament on topics related to Hinduism, Buddhism and harmony of religions. The parliament ended on 27 September 1893. All his speeches at the Parliament had the common theme of universality, and emphasised religious tolerance.

Swami Vivekananda told, we must not only tolerate other religions, but positively embrace them, and that the truth is the basis of all religions.

In several of his speeches and writings Swami Vivekananda has spoken of Universal Religion as the one Eternal Religion, representing the religious consciousness of humanity, which manifests itself in different places as different religions. Just as science is one, so also religion is one. In his famous lecture on 'My Master', Swamiji said, 'The second idea that I learnt from my Master, and which is perhaps the most vital, is the wonderful truth that the religions of the world are not contradictory or antagonistic. They are but various phases of one Eternal Religion. That one Eternal Religion is applied to different planes of existence, is applied to the opinions of various minds and various races. There never was my religion or yours.... One infinite religion existed all through eternity and will ever exist, and this religion is expressing itself in various countries in various ways.'[5]

Vivekananda talked about concept of Karma Yoga. The word Karma is derived from the Sanskrit "*Kri*", to do; all actionis *Karma*. Technically, this word also means the effects of actions. In connection with metaphysics, it sometimes means the effects, of which our past actions were the causes. But in Karma Yoga, wehave simply to do with the word Karma as meaning work. Thegoal of mankind is knowledge. That is the one ideal placed beforeus by Eastern philosophy. Pleasure is not the goal of man, but knowledge. Pleasure and happiness come to an end. It is a mistake to suppose that pleasure is the goal. The cause of all the miseries,we have in the world is that men foolishly think pleasure to be the ideal to strive for. After a time man finds that it is not happiness, but knowledge, towards which he is going, and that both pleasure and pain are great teachers, and that he learns as much from evilas from good. As pleasure and pain pass before his soul they have upon it different pictures, and the result of these combined impressions is what is called man's "character". If you take the character of any man, it really is but the aggregate of tendencies, the sum total of the bent of his mind. You will find that misery and happiness are equal factors in the formation of that character. Good and evil have an equal share in moldings character, and insome instances misery is a greater teacher than happiness. In studying the great characters the world has produced, I dare say, in the vast majority of cases. It would be found that it was misery that taught more than happiness, it was poverty that taught more than wealth, it was blows that brought out their inner fire more than praise.

Education

Swami Vivekananda believed education is the manifestation of perfection already in men. He thought it a pity that the existing system of education did not enable a person to stand on his own feet, nor did it teach him self-confidence and self-respect. To Vivekananda, education was not only collection of information, but also something more meaningful; he felt education should be man-making, life giving and character-building. To him education was an assimilation of noble ideas.

"Education is not the amount of information that we put into your brain and runs riot there, undigested, all your life. We must have life building, man making, and character making assimilation of ideas. If you have assimilated five ideas and made them your life and character, you have

more education than any man who has got by heart a whole library…"

Swami Vivekananda stressed on giving the public only positive education, because negative thoughts weaken men. Swami Vivekananda told, if young boys and girls are encouraged and are not unnecessarily criticised all the time, they are bound to improve in time. In New York, Vivekananda used to observe the Irish colonists come - downtrodden, haggard-looking, destitute of all possessions at home, penniless, and wooden-headed - with their only belongings, a stick and a bundle of rags hanging at the end of it, fright in their steps, alarm in their eyes. Vivekananda observed a completely different spectacle in next six months—the man walks upright, his attire is changed. In his eyes and steps there is more fright. Swami Vivekananda tried to find out the cause, he told, if this incidence is seen by the explanations of Vedanta, that Irish man was kept surrounded by contempt in his own country - the whole of Nature was telling him with one voice - "Pat, you have no more hope, you were born a slave and will remain so". Having been thus told from his birth, Pat started believing in it and hypnotised himself that he is very low. While no sooner had he landed on America than the shout went up on all sided - "Pat, you are a man as we are, it is man who has done all, a man like you and me can do everything; have courage!" Pat raised his head and saw that it was so; the self-confidence within him woke up again. Swami Vivekananda feels likewise, the education that young boys and girls receive is very negative. He thinks they do not gain confidence or self-respect from this education, so according to Swami Vivekananda only positive education should be given to children.[6]

Swami Vivekananda was always supportive for the education which builds character. According to him, The king now has nothing to say in any social matter; on the other hand, the Indian people have not yet even the least faith in themselves, what to say of self-reliance. The faith in one's own Self, which is the basis of Vedânta, has not yet been even slightly carried into practice. It is for this reason that the Western method—i.e. first of all, discussion about the wished-for end, then the carrying it out by the combination of all the forces—is of no avail even now in this country: it is for this reason that we appear so greatly conservative under foreign rule. If this be true, then it is a vain attempt to do any great work by means of public discussion. "There is no chance of a headache where there is no head"—where is the public? Besides, we are so devoid of strength that our whole energy is exhausted if we undertake to discuss anything, none is left for work. It is for this reason, I suppose, we observe in Bengal almost always — "Much cry but little wool." Secondly, as I have written before, I do not expect anything from the rich people of India. It is best to work among the youth in whom lies our hope—patiently, steadily, and without noise".[7]

Swamiji asked downtrodden section of society that education is the only medium of liberation. Education, education, education alone! Travelling through many cities of Europe and observing in them the comforts and education of even the poor people, there was brought to my mind the state of our own poor people, and I used to shed tears. What made the difference? Education was the answer I got. Through education comes faith in one's own Self, and through faith in one's own Self the inherent Brahman is waking up in them, while the Brahman in us is gradually becoming dormant. In New York I used to observe the Irish colonists come—downtrodden, haggard-looking, destitute of all possessions at home, penniless, and wooden-headed—with their only belongings, a stick and a bundle of rags hanging at the end of it, fright in their steps, alarm in their eyes. A different spectacle in six months—the man walks upright, his attire is changed! In his eyes and steps there is no more sign of fright. What is the cause? Our Vedanta says that that Irishman was kept surrounded by contempt in his own country—the whole of nature was telling him with one voice, "Pat, you have no more hope, you are born a slave and will remain so." Having been thus told from his birth, Pat believed in it and hypnotised himself that he was very low, and the Brahman in him shrank away. While no sooner had he landed in America than he heard the shout going up on all sides, "Pat, you are a man as we are. It is man who has done all, a man like you and me can do everything: have courage!" Pat raised his head and saw that it was so, the Brahman within woke up. Nature herself spoke, as it were, "Arise, awake, and stop not till the goal is reached" (Katha Upanishad, I. ii. 4.)

Sister Nivedita used to say that those who knew Swami Vivekananda understood that he was one who had experienced in his own life all the truths about which he spoke. This is equally valid when he addressed the subject of education. To him education plays a vital role in curing the evils in society, and it is critical in shaping the future of humanity. Although Vivekananda did not write a book on education, he contributedvaluable thoughts on the subject that are relevant and viable today. In order to understand his thoughts, we should first consider his oft-quoted definition of education – 'Education is the manifestation of the perfection already in man'.[8]

Education, he said, must provide 'life-building, man-making, character-making assimilation of ideas'. The ideal of this type of education would be to produce an integrated person–one who has learned how to improve his intellect, purify his emotions, and stand firm on moral virtues and unselfishness. There are two levels designated by the ancient Indian scriptures as paravidya (spiritual values) and aparavidya (secular values) respectively. This division is merely for practical convenience; otherwise Vidya, or learning, is a continuum, leading one towards the ultimate goal, which according to Vivekananda, was complete freedom of the soul. Vivekananda also observed that, if education is to serve the entire human being, in all his/her dimensions.The pursuit of knowledge will be a lifelong process. Even an illustrious being like Sri Ramakrishna said, from his own experience, 'As long as I live, so long do I learn.' At the empirical level, today's knowledge explosion can keep people engaged for their entire lives. Therefore, education must be considered a continuous and lifelong process. So far, our discussion of Vivekananda's ideas on education has been a simplistic analysis centering round his definition of education. However, this fails to do justiceto some of his ideas on related issues, such as the relationship between education and society, between education and the teacher, between the professed goals of education and the goals actually achieved, and so forth. It is apparent, therefore, that Vivekananda's deep concern for social justice has not been reflected so far in our definition.

Vivekananda observed that, through education, a child learns a culture and his behaviour is moulded accordingly, and he is thus guided towards his eventual role in society. In this process, several agents - such as his parents, peers and teachers - assist him. But nowadays, as formal education has become more and more institutionalised, teachers are expected to play a more significant role. A teacher needs to help a student learn how to think, what to think, how to discriminate and how to appreciate things. This is not just a matter of intellectual manipulation. This kind of teaching requires moral conviction and the courage to continuously pursue one's own course at all costs. The teacher must not only possess the knowledge he is to transmit to the student, but he must also know how to transmit it. And, in addition to the content of the teaching, what the teacher gives or transfers, to be truly effective, must possess some other elements. For instance, the teacher should share with the student the conviction that they are both truly one in Spirit – at the same time cultivating in the student a feeling of dignity and self-respect. As Vivekananda said:

"*The only true teacher is he who can immediately come down to the level of the student, and transfer his soul to the student's soul and see through the student's eyes and hear through his ears and understand through his mind. Such a teacher can really teach and none else*"[11].

So far we have discussed education primarily in the context of the society that already benefits from education. Vivekananda, however, was a genuine friend of the poor and the weak, particularly the helpless masses of India, and he was the first Indian leader who sought a solution to their problems through education. He argued that a nation was advanced to the extent that education and culture reached the masses. Unless there was uniform circulation of national blood all over the body, the nation could not rise. He insisted that it was the duty of the upper classes, who had received their education at the expense of the poor, to come forward and uplift the poor through education and other means. In fact, the Swami's mission was for the poor.

He once said, 'there must be equal chance for all – or if greater for some and for some less – the weaker should be given more chance than the strong'.The trend in recent years has been to shift the responsibility for education from the family, religious institutions, private charities and so forth, to public authorities, particularly the State. Yet, in spite of this shift to the State, education has hardly reached the most under privileged. As they are often victims of malnutrition, poor hygienic conditions and overcrowded housing, they can hardly take advantage of any half-hearted opportunity that is offered. Vivekananda felt that alienation of any kind from the masses of society, who are mostly poor - whether it be alienation through learning, through wealth or through force of arms - weakens the leadership of a country. Therefore, for a sustainable regeneration of India, if not for anything else, top priority must be given to educating the masses and restoring to them their lost individuality. They should not only be given education to make them self-reliant, but also ideas, moral training and an understanding of their own historical situation so that they can work out their own salvation. Furthermore, they must be given culture, without which there can be no hopefor their long-term progress.

The Swami was particularly worried about the degradation of women in India. He was emphatic that women must be educated, for he believed that it is the women who mould the next generation, and hence, the destiny of the country. In Vivekananda's educational scheme for India, the uplift of women and the masses received the highest priority, and his ideas approximated to Paulo Freire's concept of 'Conscientisation'.

Womanhood

Swami Vivekananda warned, it is completely unfair to discriminate between sexes, as there is not any sex distinction in *atman* (soul), the soul has neither sex, nor caste nor imperfection. He suggested not to think that there are men and women, but only that there are human beings. Swami Vivekananda felt, the best thermometer to the progress of a nation is its treatment of its women. It is impossible to get back India's lost pride and honor unless they try to better the condition of women. Vivekananda considered men and women as two wings of a bird, and it is not possible for a bird to fly on only one wing. So, according to him, there is no chance for welfare of the world unless the condition of woman is improved.

Swami Vivekananda noticed almost everywhere women are treated as playthings. In modern countries like America, women have more independence, still, Vivekananda had noticed, men bow low, offer a woman a chair and in another breath they offer compliments like "Oh, how beautiful your eyes. . . " etc. Vivekananda felt, a man does not have any right to do this or venture so far, and any woman should not permit this as well. According to Swami Vivekananda such things develop the less noble side of humanity. They do not tend to noble ideals.[9]

According to Swami Vivekananda, Sita is typical of India – the idealised India. Swami Vivekananda assured if world literature of the past and world literature of the future are thoroughly exhausted..Yet, it'll not be possible to find out another Sita, because Sita is unique, the character was depicted once for all. Swami Vivekananda felt there may have been several Ramas, perhaps, but never more than one Sita. Sita was a true Indian by nature, Vivekananda concluded, who never returned injury.

1. ***Identity:*** It was Swami Vivekananda who gave to Hinduism as a whole a clear-cut identity, a distinct profile. Before Swamiji came Hinduism was a loose confederation of many different sects. Swamiji was the first religious leader to speak about the common bases of Hinduism and the common ground of all sects. He was the first person, as guided by his Master Sri Ramakrishna, to accept all Hindu doctrines and the views of all Hindu philosophers and sects as different aspects of one total view of Reality and way of life known as Hinduism. Speaking about Swamiji's role in giving Hinduism its distinct identity, **Sister Nivedita** wrote— "... it may be said that when he began to

speak it was of 'the religious ideas of the Hindus', but when he ended, Hinduism had been created."

2. ***Unification:*** Before Swamiji came; there was a lot of quarrel and competition among the various sects of Hinduism. Similarly, the protagonists of different systems and schools of philosophy were claiming their views to be the only true and valid ones. By applying Sri Ramakrishna's doctrine of Harmony (Samanvaya) Swamiji brought about an overall unification of Hinduism on the basis of the principle of unity in diversity. Speaking about Swamiji's role in this field **K. M. Pannikar**, the eminent historian and diplomat, wrote, "This new Shankaracharya may well be claimed to be a unifier of Hindu ideology."

3. ***Defence:*** Another important service rendered by Swamiji was to raise his voice in defence of Hinduism. In fact, this was one of the main types of work he did in the West. Christian missionary propaganda had given a wrong understanding of Hinduism and India in Western minds. Swamiji had to face a lot of opposition in his attempts to defend Hinduism.

4. ***Meeting the Challenges:*** At the end of the 19th century, India in general, and Hinduism in particular, faced grave challenges from Western materialistic life. The ideas of Western free society, and the proselytizing activities of Christians. Vivekananda met these challenges by integrating the best elements of Western culture in Hindu culture.

5. ***New Ideal of Monasticism:*** A major contribution of Vivekananda to Hinduism is the rejuvenation and modernisation of monasticism. In this new monastic ideal, followed in the Ramakrishna order, the ancient principles of renunciation and God realisation are

combined with service to God in man (*Shiva jnanejivaseva*). Vivekananda elevated social service to the status of divine service.

6. ***Refurbishing of Hindu Philosophy and Religious Doctrines:*** Vivekananda did not merely interpret ancient Hindu scriptures and philosophical ideas in terms of modern thought. He also added several illuminating original concepts based on his own transcendental experiences and vision of the future. This, however, needs a detailed study of Hindu philosophy, which cannot be attempted here.

Conclusion

Vivekananda revitalised Hinduism within and outside India. He was the principal reason behind the enthusiastic reception of yoga, transcendental meditation and other forms of Indian spiritual self-improvement in the West. Professor Agehananda Bharati explained that, "...modern Hindus derive their knowledge of Hinduism from Vivekananda, directly or indirectly." Vivekananda espoused the idea that all sects within Hinduism and, indeed, all religions, are different paths to the same goal. This view, however, has been criticised for over simplification of Hinduism.

The first governor general of independent India, Chakravarti Rajagopalachari said "Vivekananda saved Hinduism, saved India." According to Subhas Chandra Bose, a major proponent of armed struggle for Indian independence, Vivekananda was "the maker of modern India"; for Mahatma Gandhi, Vivekananda's influence increased his "love for his country a thousand fold." Vivekananda influenced India's independence movement; his writings inspired a whole generation of freedom fighters such as Netaji Subhas Chandra Bose, Aurobindo Ghose, Bal Gangadhar Tilak and Bagha Jatin. Many years after Vivekananda's death, Rabindranath

Tagore told French Nobel Laureate Romain Rolland, "If you want to know India, study Vivekananda. In him everything is positive and nothing negative." Rolland himself wrote that "His words are great music, phrases in the style of Beethoven, stirring rhythms like the march of Händel choruses. I cannot touch these sayings of his, scattered as they are through the pages of books, at thirty years' distance, without receiving a thrill through my body like an electric shock. And what shocks, what transports, must have been produced when in burning words they issued from the lips of the hero!" Swami Vivekananda's contribution to Hinduism has been immense.

References

1. Vivekananda, Swami (2010), *Complete Works of Swami Vivekananda*, Volume 9, pp. 178–179, Advaita Ashrama.
2. Dhar, Shailendra Nath (1976), *A Comprehensive Biography of Swami Vivekananda* (2 ed.), Madras, India: Vivekananda Prakashan Kendra, pp. 121–123.
3. Kashyap, Shivendra (2012), *Saving Humanity: Swami Vivekanand Perspective*, Vivekanand Swadhyay Mandal, pp. 43–44.
4. *"The Complete Works of Swami Vivekananda,* Volume 5, Advaita Ashrama, p. 90.
5. "*The Complete Works of Swami Vivekananda*, Volume 1, Advaita Ashrama, p. 24.
6. "*The Complete Works of Swami Vivekananda, Volume* 4, Advaita Ashrama, p. 23.
7. *The Complete Works of Swami Vivekananda, Volume* 4, Advaita Ashrama, p. 258.
8. *The Complete Works of Swami Vivekananda, Volume* 3, Advaita Ashrama, p. 302.
9. Vivekananda, Swami (1996). *My India: the India eternal* (1st ed.). Calcutta: Ramakrishna Mission Institute of Culture, pp. 68–69.
10. Swami Yogeshananda. "A Vedantist's View of Mary", http://www.vedanta-atlanta.org.
11. *The Complete Works of Swami Vivekananda, Volume* 4, Advaita Ashrama, p. 183.

4

Relevance of Swami Vivekananda in Contemporary Times

Naved Jamal

Basically, Swami Vivekananda Alias Narendranath Datta (12 January 1863 - 4 July 1902) is a great philosopher, thinker, saint and spiritual monk but we can see his relevance in social sciences in general and political science and sociology in particular. His ideas are vivid and vibrant related to spirituality, ethics, theology and even real problems of life. Swamiji not only saw the problems of life and society but he also presented the solution of the problems and that is the main reason that makes Swamiji relevant and significant in contemporary times. Swami Vivekananda was deeply interested in uncovering the creative understanding of Indian ethos, culture and civilisation since his childhood. With his impeccable travelling zeal, he spread the spirit of enlightenment in India and across the globe.

Swami Vivekananda recognised and uncovered the vices within the societal structure and brings in the scientific ethos and humanism to eradicate them. The intermingling of science with spirituality led to a new wave of knowledge as power. The understanding of India as a great civilisation was quintessentially germane to his thought in terms of realisation of philosophical roots and realistic worldview. The relevance of his ideas in contemporary times among youth has more profound effect. The recognition and empowerment of women and youth is the sine qua non of equality with modern philosophical underpinnings. The confluence of civilisational aspect with cultural dialogue with the West became a significant hallmark of his philosophy.

He was meticulous, generous and devoted to serve the humanity and wanted to give the human civilization a new and peaceful dimension. He came into the contact of Ramakrishna, became highly influential to him, and later became one of the greatest disciple of Ramakrishna Pramhans and chief architect of Ramakrishna mission, the founder of the Ramakrishna Math. After the death of his guru, he travelled Indian subcontinent to acquire the first hand knowledge. Thereafter he went America to attend Parliament of World Religion where he received wider popularity. His uniqueness in the presentation 'Sister and Brother of America' got wider appreciation drew the warmly attention of all the delegates. After this lecture, he started to deliver lecture in country to country. He spent about five years in the United States of America and other western countries and gave 317 talks, 431 small group talks and participated in 26 discussion panels, introduces Hinduism and opened the treasures of Vedanta to the Western mind and it was continued till the end of his last breath.

Throughout the life and his teaching, he delivered the sermon for the peaceful coexistence of the world civilization. However, he was known Hindu Indian religious pioneering philosopher but he always talked about the mankind. The idea of India as a distinct civilisation and cultural habitat found its most creative expression in Swami Vivekananda. It was his persistent belief that India was capable of giving back to the world as much as it took from the world and thereby re-establish its rightful claim in the assembly of nations.[1] Up until the 18th century, the term "civilization" described the opposite of barbarism. Today it has gained a new meaning as a virtual synonym for culture and society. An American scholar, Samuel P. Huntington's definition of a civilization is similar: "A civilization is a cultural entity the highest cultural grouping of people and the broadest level of cultural identity people have."[2] According to Huntington, "the great divisions of mankind and the dominating source of conflict will be cultural."[3] In response, it was stressed that the main virtue of the Alliance of Civilizations another initiative towards peace in comparison to other, similar initiatives was that it did not remain in getting to know each other in order to overcome stereotypes and mutual hostility, but that it aimed at urging concrete measures of common action beyond simple exchange. This difference, it was stated, was also perceived at the United Nations Headquarters, and had even been recognized by initiators of other initiatives, like the aforementioned Dialogue of Civilizations led by Syed Mohammad Khatami. The Dialogue and Alliance of Civilizations has opened a door but has been practically exhausted, so now it is time to start a new impulse with a different strategy based on the ideas of Swami Vivekananda.

Swami Vivekananda while addressing at the Parliament of Religions in second session at Chicago explained through a little story of frogs, the confluence of cultures and civilisation. Both civilizations were asserted to have stereotyped images of the other, and that religion, as well as imperial dominance in the past and present, played important roles in this regard. Stereotypes must be cleaned up through massive means, and that the culture of confrontation arising from it must be counteracted.

However, in reality Huntington's theory has had a highly unconstructive effect on public discourse, poisoning public debate and people's minds for over two decades with ideas that have been feeding hostile attitudes. Looking at how negative perceptions in both civilizations are created and nourished, the role of public political debate and especially the mass media was strongly emphasized. Both civilizations, people live in an atmosphere which was denominated "ideology of fear": a wanted strategy to make people fear the other and maintain conflictive perceptions.

According to prominent Orientalist, Edward Said, "the real question is whether in the end we want to work for civilizations that are separate, or whether we should be taking the more integrative, but perhaps more difficult path, which is to see them as making one vast whole, whose exact contours are impossible for any person to grasp, but whose certain existence we can intuit and feel and study."[4] In this important lecture delivered at the University of Massachusetts, Said takes aim at one of the central tenets of recent foreign policy thinking— that conflicts between different and "clashing civilizations" (Western, Islamic, Confucian) characterize the contemporary world.

Huntington's theory had been granted too much scientific significance, and was best opposed by ignoring it. However, in practice, the theory has attracted vast attention, and no matter to what degree one might consider the "clash of civilizations" to reflect current realities, there is no doubt that it has been successfully used in Western political discourse.

Tapan Raychaudhuri's article on "Swami Vivekananda's Construction of Hinduism", argued that any attempt to present Vivekananda as a Hindu fundamentalist or communalist grossly contradicts the evidence. Rather, argues Ray Chaudhuri, the Swami's concerns were (1) his personal quest for realization following the discipline of Ramakrishna, (2) at Chicago he countered the then popular Western view of Hinduism as a form of barbarism, and (3) the national revival of India in which the monks and nuns of the Ramakrishna Order were to play a central role (with the monistic doctrine of Vedanta as the key inspiration for this activity). In this context Vivekananda rejected all narrow forms of Hindu revival.[5] Future Indians, said Vivekananda, were to have strong Muslim bodies and Vedantic souls. In his nationalist vision, he claimed the Indo-Islamic poet as part of India's heritage. Ray Chaudhuri makes a strong case for the deep chasm between Vivekananda's deep revulsion for many of the fundamentalists of Brahmanical Hinduism and his programme to revive India by feedings, healing, and educating the masses - Hindus and Muslims alike, says Ray Chaudhuri.

In the modern times world is passing through transitional phase from feudal/ agriculture to industrial - informational. He realised, in this age, humankind is passing in the big crisis. Use and abuse of technological advancement are on rampant everywhere. This fast changing world, scientific and mechanical development, made the man like a machine than a human. This technological advancement, some extent, is undermining the moral and religious values, fundamental principles of civilization are being ignored. Although he was not against the technological advancement but he wanted to proper application of technology that could serve entire humanity rather individual interest.

At this time people are being used as a commodity rather than human, resources are being synchronising in the particular hand. Conflict of ideas, manner and habit are pervading the atmosphere. He realised the solution of these social and global evils is education.

According to Vivekananda, education should be given moral and value based and have a particular aim that could serve the entire humanity cutting across the religious and geographical boundaries'. His life and teaching were full of philosophy. His teachings were modern, rational and universal and applicable to all people without any discrimination on the basis of caste, colour, religion, race and the occupation. This precious teaching enables young people to lead the moral and spiritual life, and attain true fulfilment and peace of life. His ideas have become highly influential across the culture and civilization and provided the new roadmap to the people, especially youth, to achieve the success, peace, prosperity and happiness. These ideas brought new paradigm shift across the world and peeped the path of interfaith awareness among the world. The powerful teachings of Swami Vivekananda infuse the self-confidence and inner strength to the face the multiples problems at the every walk of life, people face.

Vivekananda modernization meant both physical and mental reform. "His central project - uniting his work in India and the West - was to work out what in the religious traditions not only of India but of all countries and civilizations was valid and acceptable to modern scientific and historical understanding: What should be preserved from the past and what should be discarded from the world's religions? These questions are as crucial today as they were a hundred years ago.[6]

Historically, the terms "East" and "West" arose from the split of the Christian Church in the Roman Empires of the West and East, thus out of a break within Christianity. A clear image of the other, as well as of one's own identity, is pre conditions for recognizing and respecting each other's differences. When talking about Swami Vivekananda, he builds a bridge between the Indian and Western culture with incorporation of science, technology and humanism with spirituality. What constitutes "the West"? The quest for an entity called "the West", in order to find a term one can actually operate with, does not prove much easier. Swamiji opened new avenues for the India, thus ended cultural isolation.

Western civilization in the modern times is dominating on the global culture and facing multiple criticisms. Vivekananda attitude towards western material culture was partly negative and partly supportive. He supported the merit of materialism but argued that superiority of spiritualism should be over materialism. He said, "Hail Columbia, motherland of liberty! It has been given to thee, who never dipped her hand in her neighbour's blood, who never found out that the shortest way of becoming rich was by robbing one's neighbours, it has been given to thee to march at the vanguard of civilization with the flag of harmony."[7]

He explored the spiritual culture of India at a global platform and recounted the importance of centuries old civilisation. He distinguished that religion survives on the belief while spirituality comes through inner practices. This spirituality lays the foundation of global cultural human based civilisation. For the strengthening of global humanity, he led the foundation of Vedanta society in New York in 1894 with motto of to provide the moral and value based education to all, in America.

We live in an era of a re-enchantment of the world, a parallel spreading of technology and religion through globalisation, through which religion seems to live a comeback. But the revert to religion is not a return. What returns is not religion, but religious practices. Herein Swamiji urged Spirituality. Globally speaking, there is an increasing social pressure to exercise religious practices, mostly transmitted by the media and boosted by the process of globalisation, resulting in a "merchandization" of religion. American neo-liberalism supports the revival of religion in the US, but in fact it is not a real religious comeback but a political recourse to the religious as a means to secure imperial dominance. But for Swami Vivekananda, religion is the manifestation of divinity already existing in man.[8] For Vivekananda, the road to good us the roughest and steepest in universe. It is a wonder that so many succeed no wonder that so many fall. Character has to be established through thousand stumbles.[9]

Fusion of Philosophy and Real Life

Swamiji was not a mere philosopher though he tried to conclude philosophy, ethics and morality and made useful to transcendental and epistemological knowledge so that we can solve the problems of our life. In Western tradition of philosophy, catalyst element of knowledge gain is curiosity. In West, philosophy was either rationalist, imperialist, the Kantian review or idealistic dialect of Hegel rarely able to solve the problems of real life. Even Hegel's philosophy made so much rationality that in the reaction of those philosophies existentialism has arisen to solve basic problems of life on some instincts. On the other hand, Swamiji enriched the tradition of Indian philosophy in which every philosophy has its own ethical and moral code. Either it is Buddhism, Jainism, or six schools of philosophy; they all have concentrated on moral system and to eradicate the sorrow of life.

In the same vein, Swamiji was the philosopher of *Advait Vedanta*. He saw the main reason of sorrow is *agyanya* (ignorance). Swami Vivekananda saw that in India it is *Agyanya* that distorted the religion make it *Karmkandia* (liturgical) and orthodox. Secondly, he saw because of *agyanya*, Indians have lost their self confidence and the people don't know about the nation, national pride and motherhood. It's because of this factor Indians were colonised by the Britishers. Thirdly, Swamiji found that due to *Agyanya*, people don't have the basic knowledge and skills, to earn their livelihood so as to fulfil and accomplish their basic needs.

Distorted Face of Religion: Then and Now

Swamiji evidenced Karmkand (liturgical) and orthodox trends and bad practices in religion spread in Indian society. During his Bharat darshan, he delivered many lectures to come out from liturgical act and orthodox mindset. For Swamiji, religion was not a tradition or compulsion. Although, he carried religion as a moral system and believe that religion will be able to give internal inspiration. He always use to see in society that religion is being practiced between people as a tradition or a compulsion instead of a moral system. People follow religion because of fear of God not because of love of God. Swamiji gave lectures during his Chicago visit to stimulate and motivate people for love of God (Ishprem). Today, when religion has been captured by orthodox people and extremists and religion has lost its progressive form, it has fallen from the level of knowledge and truth. Swamiji considered religion as a means of knowledge. He considered religion as a tool of development. He expressed great sorrow on the narrowness of religion because he was an ardent admirer of interreligious communication and dialogue and coexistence of religions. On this topic, in Chicago, Swamiji gave an example of frogs of well. He said, "I will tell you a little story". You have heard the eloquent speaker who has just finished say, "Let us cease from abusing each other," and he was very sorry that there should be always so much variance.

He said, "But I think I should tell you a story which would illustrate the cause of this variance. A frog lived in a well. It had lived there for a long time. It was born there and brought up there, and yet was a little, small frog. Of course the evolutionists were not there then to tell us whether the frog lost its eyes or not, but, for our story's sake, we must take it for granted that it had its eyes, and that it every day cleansed the water of all the worms and bacilli that lived in it with an energy that would do credit to our modern bacteriologists. In this way it went on and became a little sleek and fat. Well, one day another frog that lived in the sea came and fell into the well.

"Where are you from?"

"I am from the sea."

"The sea! How big is that? Is it as big as my well?" and he took a leap from one side of the well to the other.

"My friend," said the frog of the sea, "how do you compare the sea with your little well?"

Then the frog took another leap and asked, "Is your sea so big?"

"What nonsense you speak, to compare the sea with your well!"

"Well, then," said the frog of the well, "nothing can be bigger than my well; there can be nothing bigger than this; this fellow is a liar, so turn him out."

That has been the difficulty all the while.

He further explained that "I am a Hindu. I am sitting in my own little well and thinking that the whole world is my little well. The Christian sits in his little well and thinks the whole world is his well. The Mohammedan sits in his little well and thinks that is the whole world. I have to thank you of America for the great attempt you are making to break down the barriers of this little world of ours, and hope that, in the future, the Lord will help you to accomplish your purpose.[10]

At the final and sixth session of the Chicago Address, Vivekananda said, "the seed is put in the ground, and earth and air and water are placed around it." Does the seed become the earth, or the air, or the water? No. It becomes a plant, it develops after the law of its own growth, assimilates the air, the earth, and the water, converts them into plant substance, and grows into a plant. Similar is the case with religion. The Christian is not to become a Hindu or a Buddhist, nor a Hindu or a Buddhist to become a Christian. But each must assimilate the spirit of the others and yet preserve their individuality and grow according to their own law of growth.

"Religions of the world have become lifeless mockeries. What the world wants is character. The world is in need of those whose life is one burning love, selfless. That love will make every word tell like thunderbolt," he said.[11] If the Parliament of Religions has shown anything to the world it is this: It has proved to the world that holiness, purity and charity are not the exclusive possessions of any church in the world, and that every system has produced men and women of the most exalted character. In the face of this evidence, if some people still dream of the exclusive survival of their own religion and the destruction of the others, I pity them from the bottom of my heart, and point out to them that upon the banner of every religion will soon be written, in spite of resistance: "Help and not Fight", "Assimilation and not Destruction"; "Harmony and Peace and not Dissension."[12]

He said that people having different religion as Hindu, Muslim, Christianity and other religious beliefs are living in well and does not know about the other religions. He said, religion should come out of this narrowness. In contemporary scenario, tension between religion and civilisations have increased and people and academicians are talking about Clash of Civilisation as propounded by Samuel P. Huntington, because the lack of interreligious communication and lack of knowledge about other religions.

While, Swamiji was an ardent admirer of religious plurality. He appealed to the people to come out of the religious narrowness and to learn about good things of other religions. He believes, in the honour of all religions and that is the reason Vivekananda is more relevant in contemporary times.

Fabulous Presentation of the Ideas of the East: Self Respect and National Pride

In his time, Swamiji seen that after being politically colonised, people are also slaves on cultural front. Britishers made believe between Indian people that Western culture is superior that the culture of East and India, Swamiji break this myth. On the basis of Advait Vedanta, which is the part of Vedanta tradition, raised the self confidence of Indians. He shone and shine the glorious tradition of Indian culture and Indian philosophy. Because of this, Indian recognise their prosperous culture. Due to his honour for this culture and self respect increased among the people. Further the self confidence made a great contribution for national pride and nation building.

In Chicago, Swami Vivekananda presented the Indian philosophy and ideas and break the myth of superiority of Western philosophy and culture. People of the West got informed by the Swamiji that no one culture is superior or inferior although the cultures are different ways of life and gives meaning to civilisation. Instead of talking about Clash of civilisation, we should have an honour and tolerance for every culture.

Through his whole life, Vivekananda tried to understand and develop Indian nation. After his life, he was a source of inspiration for the nationalists. Subhash Chandra Bose saw as the Pre man of nation. Although Vivekananda spent his life in the development of *Advait* and Hindu religion but basically, he applied religion and philosophy in nation building at that time.

Poverty and Serious Efforts of Swamiji

Vivekananda tried to understand nation by travelling across India. What he saw is a matter of sorrow. He saw extreme and abject poverty. He saw poverty as one of the main reason for the problems and evils in Indian scenario. Swamiji saw another difficult situation against the development of the nation that the people are peeping around the transcendental ideas. The people don't have even basic knowledge and skills to pursue their life. Finally, he found that *Agyanya* as a main source of all problems and ills of the people.

He not only discovered religion but also take serious efforts to solve the problems and ills of the society. He saw the means of spreading knowledge is education. So he forced on education and founded Ramakrishna mission for the spread of education as a serious efforts. Through his institutional efforts, he made a long lasting effect on the hearts and minds of people of India.

Religious but not Communal

The greatest attribute of ideas of Vivekananda is being involved in the discourse on Hinduism but his ideas were not limited within the boundaries of Hindu religion and he always taught to people to be broadminded.

Vivekananda always talked about equal honour for all religions. He believed that a religious person should not talk about religious supremacy of one's own religion. Although one should see different religions as a different paths to God. He represented these thoughts in Chicago lectures.

Hedonism versus Spirituality

Vivekananda showed great concern for increased hedonism. He takes these trends as directionless life. According to Swamiji, hedonism gives a joy of a moment but finally it will destroy our lives. He recognised the hidden trends of materialism as an exploiter. He saw that how materialism demands more and more for self happiness and inspire for more and more consumption. In this way of life, a person never thinks of exploitation of others for his material gains. Swamiji had seen colonial powers in the same way of hedonism. Opposite of this, spirituality inspires us internally. It teaches us self control and finally gives real life of joy. Swamiji considers internal inspiration as the most important thing that can give us direction to our life.

Materialism and Morality

We should understand the difference between physical or material and materialism. Swamiji criticized materialism but not criticized physical growth. So when he saw the poverty in India, he talks about physical growth. Swamiji did a fine balance annexation of physicality and morality. In his Chicago visit, he saw that an Indian people think in transcendental way. He said that Indians should also understand the importance of physical growth. On the other hand, he shows anxiousness on the West where they turned in hedonism and materialism. He said that West has recognized the importance of physical growth but now it turned toward hedonism and materialism. Finally, he talks about the balance between physical and moral growth on both places.

Women Issues and Swamiji

Swamiji was a philosopher of *Advaita Vedanta* and for him there was no discrimination between male and female. Therefore any kind of gender discrimination was unforgivable for him. In his explanation, Swamiji encourage the ancient women and their work along with giving huge importance to women respect. However, Swamiji also appeal to understand the women and their related issues in relation with their culture.

In relation if we see, on one side, Swamiji talks about women empowerment and their importance while on the other hand, he said, to understand the situation of women in relation with their culture. In recent times, feminism talks, understanding women in their cultural reference is given importance.

In short, the life and work of Swami Vivekananda mark the historical and philosophical process of India and across globe finding a due place in the modern industrial times. These are also emblematic of the way in which a tradition modernises or creates alternative forms of modernity.

Swami Vivekananda's contributions, known in many sense, profoundly shaped the perspective of intellectuals in India and the West. These insights included the necessity of equal respect for all religions; advocacy and service for the poor and dispossessed; championing of women's rights to education and leadership; and a call to spiritual liberation for the world and national liberty for India.

Similarly, the urge and need for the idea to form Confluence, Alliance, Convergence, Conversing or Dialogue of and among Civilizations was a certain doubt on whether and in which way this would provide an added value to the field of already existing initiatives aimed at building bridges and establishing ties between different countries, peoples and cultures is an important preposition in emergent global village. While in the age of 21st century when world is facing biggest crisis, Swami Vivekananda's pioneering philosophy may have great relevance.

References

1. A.P. Sen "Remembering Vivekananda", *Frontline*, Volume 30, Issue 02, Jan. 26–Feb. 08, 2013. http://www.frontline.in/static/html/fl3002/stories/20130208300200400.htm
2. Huntington, Samuel P. "The Clash of Civilizations?" *Foreign Affairs*, no. 3, 1993.
3. *Ibid.*
4. Edward Said, The Myth of 'the Clash of Civilizations' see at http://www.mediaed.org/cgi-bin/commerce.cgi?preadd=action&key=404 Retrieved on 9-5-13.
5. William Radice, *Swami Vivekananda and the Modernization of Hinduism*, SOAS Studies on South Asia, New Delhi: Oxford University Press, 1999.
6. *Ibid.*, William Radice, *Swami Vivekananda and the Modernisation of Hinduism* p. ix.
7. Narasingha P. Sil, *Swami Vivekananda: A Reassessment*, Susquehanna University Press, 1997, p. 65.
8. *The Complete Works of Swami Vivekananda*, Vol. 3, Calcutta, Advaita Asharama, 1989, p. 482.
9. *The Complete Works of Swami Vivekananda*, Vol. 8, Calcutta, Advaita Asharama, 1989. p. 383.
10. *Why We Disagree*, Swami Vivekananda, 15 Sep. 1893.
11. Narasingha P. Sil , Swami Vivekananda: a reassessment, Susquehanna University Press, 1997, p. 76.
12. http://www.belurmath.org/swamivivekananda_works.htm.

5

Swami Vivekananda and His Philosophy

Deepak Yadav

Early life

Teachings and philosophy of Swami Vivekananda stressed on different aspects of religion, education, character building as well as social issues pertaining to India. Vivekananda was a Hindu monk from India who played significant role in introducing Vedanta to the Western world and also reviving and redefining certain aspect of the religion within India. Rabindranath Tagore commented about Swami Vivekananda and his teachings, "If you want to know India, study Vivekananda. In him everything is positive and nothing negative." Vivekananda realised a country's future depends on its people, so he mainly stressed on man, "man-making is my mission", that's how he described his teaching.[1] Vivekananda put his real ideals in few words and that was: "to preach unto mankind their divinity, and how to make it manifest in every movement of life".

Swami Vivekananda, known in his pre-monastic life as Narendra Nath Datta, was born in an affluent family in

Kolkata on 12 January 1863. His father, Vishwanath Datta, was a successful attorney with interests in a wide range of subjects, and his mother, Bhuvaneshwari Devi, was endowed with deep devotion, strong character and other qualities. A precocious boy, Narendra excelled in music, gymnastics and studies. By the time he graduated from Calcutta University, he had acquired a vast knowledge of different subjects, especially Western philosophy and history. Born with a yogic temperament, he used to practise meditation even from his boyhood, and was associated with Brahmo Movement for some time.

Narendra had developed peculiar sharpness of perception and assimilation that helped him pick up 'many gems' from the talks of Sri Rama Krishna. He could, as compared to others, easily 'see' the deep meaning in the words of Sri Rama Krishna, even though Sri Rama Krishna told them in simple language, and never as a preaching. Thus, gradually Swami Vivekananda started assimilating tips and hints on practical Vedanta that could benefit individual and collective life in society.[2]

Discovery of Real India

During his travels all over India, Swami Vivekananda was deeply moved to see the appalling poverty and backwardness of the masses. He was the first religious leader in India to understand and openly declare that the real cause of India's downfall was the neglect of the masses. The immediate need was to provide food and other bare necessities of life to the hungry millions. For this they should be taught improved methods of agriculture, village industries, etc. It was in this context that Vivekananda grasped the crux of the problem of poverty in India (which had escaped the attention of social reformers of his days), owing to centuries of oppression, the downtrodden masses had lost faith in their capacity to improve their lot. It was first of all necessary to infuse into their minds faith in themselves. For this they needed a life-giving, inspiring message. Swamiji found this message in the principle of the Atman, the doctrine of the potential divinity of the soul, taught in Vedanta, the ancient system of religious philosophy of India. He saw that, in spite of poverty, the masses clung to religion, but they had never been taught the life giving, ennobling principles of Vedanta and how to apply them in practical life.Thus the masses needed two kinds of knowledge: secular knowledge to improve their economic condition, and spiritual knowledge to infuse in them faith in themselves and strengthen their moral sense. The next question was, how to spread these two kinds of knowledge among the masses? Through education – this was the answer that Swamiji found.

In spite of her innumerable linguistic, ethnic, historical and regional diversities, India has had from time immemorial a strong sense of cultural unity. It was, however, Swami Vivekananda who revealed the true foundations of this culture and thus clearly defined and strengthened the sense of unity as a nation.

Swamiji gave Indians proper understanding of their country's great spiritual heritage and thus gave them pride in their past. Furthermore, he pointed out to Indians the drawbacks of Western culture and the need for India's contribution to overcome these drawbacks. In this way Swamiji made India a nation with a global mission.

Sense of unity, pride in the past, sense of mission – these were the factors which gave real strength and purpose to India's nationalist movement. Several eminent leaders of India's freedom movement have acknowledged their indebtedness to Swamiji. Free India's first Prime Minister Jawaharlal Nehru wrote: "Rooted in the past, full of pride in India's prestige, Vivekananda was yet modern in his approach to life's problems, and was a kind of bridge between the past of India and her present ... he came as a tonic to the depressed and demoralised Hindu mind and gave it self-reliance and some roots in the past." Netaji Subhash Chandra Bose wrote: "Swamiji harmonised the East and the West, religion and science, past and present. And that is why he is great. Our countrymen have gained unprecedented self-respect, self-reliance and self-assertion from his teachings." Swamiji's most unique contribution to the creation of new India was to open the minds of Indians to their duty to the downtrodden masses. Long before the ideas of Karl Marx were known in India, Swamiji spoke about the role of the labouring classes in the production of the country's wealth. Swamiji was the first religious leader in India to speak for the masses, formulate a definite philosophy of service, and organise large-scale social service.

Shiva Jnane Jiva Seva (Service of Man as God) The invaluable mantra "Shiva Jnane Jiva Seva" (Serving every being as the full manifestation of God) Narendranath received from Sri Ramakrishna.

For instance, sometime in 1884, once Sri Ramakrishna was sitting in the room surrounded by his devotees including Narendranath. In the course of conversation there arose a topic on Vaishnava religion, and explaining the essence of that doctrine Sri Ramakrishna said, "That doctrine teaches that one should always be careful to observe three things, namely, a taste for God's name, kindness to all beings, and the service of co-devotees. ...One should have the conviction in one's heart that the whole universe belongs to Krishna, and therefore, one should have compassion for all beings." No sooner did Sri Ramakrishna utter the words 'compassion for all beings' than he suddenly went into ecstasy. Regaining partial normal consciousness, he continued, "Talk of compassion for beings. Insignificant creature that you are, how can you show compassion for all beings? Who are you to show compassion? You wretch, who are you to bestow it. No, no; it is not compassion to Jivas, but service to them as Shiva."

All listened to those words of Sri Ramakrishna spoken in the ecstatic mood, but none could detect and understand their hidden import at that time. It was Narendranath alone who, coming out of the room at the end of Sri Ramakrishna's ecstasy, said, "Ah, what a wonderful light have I got today from Sri Ramakrishna's words. What a new and attractive Gospel have we received today through those words of his, wherein a synthesis has been effected of sweet devotion to the Lord with Vedantic knowledge, which is generally regarded as dry austere and lacking in sympathy with the suffering of others. Whenever shall I get the opportunity I will preach this wonderful doctrine of 'Shiva Jnane Jiva Seva', serving God in each living being."

To give an example how in later life Swami Vivekananda actually put this mantra in practice, the following incidence is worth mentioning: After his return from USA, around 1898, Swami Vivekananda had acquired land at Belur and constructed the Temple of Sri Ramakrishna and the Math for *Sannyasins*. He was not keeping well and had gone to Darjeeling hill station for rest. Meanwhile plague broke out in Calcutta, and panic set in all over. People were running in fear, leaving Calcutta. Many died and there was no one to take care of the sick or dispose of the dead bodies. The news reached the broad-hearted Swami who immediately returned to Calcutta and ordered all the inmates of Belur Math to get busy in the service and care of the affected. Many of *Sannyasin* protested, 'this is not our work; Sri Ramakrishna had never told us to do social service. Our main aim is to seek God and perform *Sadhana*.' This was the argument put forward by some of the *Sannyasins*.

Swami Vivekananda thundered at them saying, "O my brothers, have you forgotten the mantra of our Sri Ramakrishna: 'Shiva Jnane Jiva Seva'. By serving human beings we are serving the highest expression of God on this earth. Love the Lord in these suffering patients. I appeal to you to come forward in this calamity and serve the living God." The monks were stunned to listen to those powerful words of their leader and many of them saw the truth therein. But someone still protested, "O Swami, from where would the money come?" To this the Swami retaliated, 'If need be, sell off the Belur Math. The money thus gathered would be put to the service of these men. I care not for home or shelter for ourselves; we are sannyasins, and we have taken the vow of poverty. Tree shade would be our roof and a loin cloth would be enough for us to cover our bodies.'

Thus were engaged all the monks, householder devotees of Sri Ramakrishna, and inmates of Belur Math in the service of the afflicted. The British authorities in their report on the epidemic had recorded that due to the timely help from the Math mortality was less and moreover, the epidemic was brought under control much quickly.

At the threshold of youth Narendra had to pass through a period of spiritual crisis when he was assailed by doubts about the existence of God. It was at that time he first heard about Sri Ramakrishna from one of his English professors at college. One day in November 1881, Narendra went to meet Sri Ramakrishna who was staying at the Kali Temple in Dakshineshwar. He straightaway asked the Master a question which he had put to several others but had received no satisfactory answer: "Sir, have you seen God?" Without a moment's hesitation, Sri Ramakrishna replied: "Yes, I have. I see Him as clearly as I see you, only in a much intenser sense." Apart from removing doubts from the mind of Narendra, Sri Ramakrishna won him over through his pure, unselfish love. Thus began a guru-disciple relationship which is quite unique in the history of spiritual masters. Narendra now became a frequent visitor to Dakshineshwar and, under the guidance of the Master, made rapid strides on the spiritual path. At Dakshineshwar, Narendra also met several young men who were devoted to Sri Ramakrishna, and they all became close friends.

Swami Vivekananda stressed on giving the public only positive education, because negative thoughts weaken men. Swami Vivekananda told, if young boys and girls are encouraged and are not unnecessarily criticised all the time, they are bound to improve in time. In New York, Vivekananda used to observe the Irish colonists come - downtrodden, haggard-looking, destitute of all possessions at home, penniless, and wooden-headed - with their only belongings, a stick and a bundle of rags hanging at the end of it, fright in their steps, alarm in their eyes. Vivekananda observed a completely different spectacle in next six months- the man walks upright, his attire is changed. In his eyes and steps there is more fright. Swami Vivekananda tried to find out the cause, he told, if this incidence is seen by the explanations of Vedanta, that Irishman was kept surrounded by contempt in his own country - the whole of Nature was telling him with one voice - "Pat, you have no more hope, you were born a slave and will remain so". Having been thus told from his birth, Pat started believing in it and hypnotised himself that he is very low. While no sooner had he landed on America than the shout went up on all sided - "Pat, you are a man as we are, it is man who has done all, a man like you and me can do everything; have courage!" Pat raised his head and saw that it was so, the self-confidence within him woke up again. Swami Vivekananda feels likewise, the education that young boys and girls receive is very negative. He thinks they do not gain confidence or self-respect from this education, so according to Swami Vivekananda only positive education should be given to children.[3]

Education, education, education alone! Travelling through many cities of Europe and observing in them the comforts and education of even the poor people, there was brought to my mind the state of our own poor people, and I used to shed tears. What made the difference? Education was the answer I got. Through education comes faith in one's own Self, and through faith in one's own Self the inherent Brahman is waking up in them, while the Brahman in us is gradually becoming dormant. In New York I used to observe the Irish colonists come — downtrodden, haggard-looking, destitute of all possessions at home, penniless, and wooden-headed — with their only belongings, a stick and a bundle of rags hanging at the end of it, fright in their steps, alarm in their eyes. A different spectacle in six months — the man walks upright, his attire is changed! In his eyes and steps there is no more sign of fright. What is the cause? Our Vedanta says that that Irishman was kept surrounded by contempt in his own country — the whole of nature was telling him with one voice, "Pat, you have no more hope, you are born a slave and will remain so." Having been thus told from his birth, Pat believed in it and hypnotised himself that he was very low, and the Brahman in him shrank away. While no sooner had he landed in America than he heard the shout going up on all sides, "Pat, you are a man as we are. It is man who has done all, a man like you and me can do everything: have courage!" Pat raised his head and saw that it was so, the Brahman within woke up. Nature herself spoke, as it were, "Arise, awake, and stop not till the goal is reached" (Katha Upanishad, I. (ii) 4.)[4]

Likewise the education that our boys receive is very negative. The schoolboy learns nothing, but has everything of his own broken down — want of Shraddhâ is the result. The Shraddha which is the keynote of the Veda and the Vedanta — the Shraddha which emboldened Nachiketâ to face Yama and question him, through which Shraddha this world moves the annihilation of that Shraddha!

"The ignorant, the man devoid of Shraddha, the doubting self runs to ruin." Therefore are we so near destruction. The remedy now is the spread of education. First of all Self-knowledge, I do not mean thereby, matted hair, staff, Kamandalu, and mountain caves which the word suggests. What do I mean then? Cannot the knowledge, by which is attained even freedom from the bondage of worldly existence, bring ordinary material prosperity? Certainly it can. Freedom, dispassion, renunciation all these are the very highest ideals, but— "Even a little of this Dharma saves one from the great fear (of birth and death)." Dualist, qualified-monist, monist, Shaiva, Vaishnava, Shâkta, even the Buddhist and the Jain and others — whatever sects have arisen in India — are all at one in this respect that infinite power is latent in this Jivatman (individualised soul); from the ant to the perfect man there is the same Âtman in all, the difference being only in manifestation. "As a farmer breaks the obstacles (to the course of water)" (Patanjali's Yoga-Sutra, Kaivalsapâda, 3). That power manifests as soon as it gets the opportunity and the right place and time. From the highest god to the meanest grass, the same power is present in all — whether manifested or not. We shall have to call forth that power by going from door to door.[5]

Secondly, along with this, education has to be imparted. That is easy to say, but how to reduce it into practice? There are thousands of unselfish, kind-hearted men in our country who has renounced everything. In the same way as they travel about and give religious instructions without any remuneration, so at least half of them can be trained as teachers or bearers of such education as we need most. For that, we want first of all a centre in the capital of each Presidency, from whence to spread slowly throughout the whole of India. Two centers have recently been started in Madras and Calcutta; there is hope of more soon. Then, the greater part of the education to the poor should be given orally; time is not yet ripe for schools. Gradually in these main centres will be taught agriculture, industry, etc., and workshops will be established for the furtherance of arts. To sell the manufactures of those workshops in Europe and America, associations will be started like those already in existence. It will be necessary to start centres for women, exactly like those for men. But you are aware how difficult that is in this country. Again, "The snake which bites must take out its own poison" — and that this is going to be is my firm conviction; the money required for these works would have to come from the West. And for that reason our religion should be preached in Europe and America. Modern science has undermined the basis of religions like Christianity. Over and above that, luxury is about to kill the religious instinct itself. Europe and America are now looking towards India with expectant ewes: this is the time for philanthropy, this is the time to occupy the hostile strongholds.

In the West, women rule; all influence and power are theirs. If bold and talented women like yourself versed in Vedanta, go to England to preach, I am sure that every year hundreds of men and women will become blessed by adopting the religion of the land of Bharata. The only woman who went over from our country was Ramâbâai; her knowledge of English, Western science and art was limited; still she surprised all. If anyone like you goes, England will be stirred, what to speak of America! If an Indian woman in Indian dress preach there the religion which fell from the lips of the Rishis of India — I see a prophetic vision — there will rise a great wave which will inundate the whole Western world. Will there be no women in the land of Maitreyi, Khanâ, Lilâvati, Sâvitri, and Ubhayabhârati, who will venture to do this? The Lord knows. England we shall conquer, England we shall possess, through the power of spirituality.

"There is no other way of salvation." Can salvation ever come by getting up meetings and societies? Our conquerors must be made *Devas* by the power of our spirituality. I am a humble mendicant, an itinerant monk; I am helpless and alone. What can I do? You have the power of wealth, intellect, and education; will you forgo this opportunity? Conquest of England, Europe, and America — this should be our one supreme Mantra at present, in it lies the well-being of the country. Expansion is the sign of life, and we must spread over the world with our spiritual ideals. Alas! This frame is poor, moreover, the physique of a Bengali; even under this labour a fatal disease has attacked it, but there is the hope:

"*A kindred spirit is or will be born out of the limitless time and populous earth to accomplish the work*" (Bhavabhuti).[6]

About vegetarian diet I have to say this — first, my Master was a vegetarian; but if he was given meat offered to the Goddess, he used to hold it up to his head. The taking of life is undoubtedly sinful; but so long as vegetable food is not made suitable to the human system through progress in chemistry, there is no other alternative but meat-eating. So long as man shall have to live a Râjasika (active) life under circumstances like the present, there is no other way except through meat-eating. It is true that the Emperor Asoka saved the lives of millions of animals by the threat of the sword; but is not the slavery of a thousand years more dreadful than that? Taking the life of a few goats as against the inability to protect the honour of one's own wife and daughter, and to save the morsels for one's children from robbing hands — which of these is more sinful? Rather let those belonging to the upper ten, who do not earn their livelihood by manual labour, not take meat; but the forcing of vegetarianism upon those who have to earn their bread by labouring day and night is one of the causes of the loss of our national freedom. Japan is an example of what good and nourishing food can do.

Teachings of Vedanta

Through the talks and stories, parables and devotional songs (*Bhajana*) concerning Sri Krishna, Radha, Gopis of Vrindavan, Mother Kali, and Chaitannya, Narendrarealised that the essence of religion was to 'realise the highest spiritual Truth' in our lives. As he was opposed and reluctant to accept idol or image worship, and believed in formless God with attributes, Sri Ramakrishna explained to him the subtle points about Brahma, Atman, and Unified Consciousness - the one without the second. Thus, Sri Ramakrishna persuaded Narendra to read to him Ashtavakra Gita and similar texts on Advaita Vedanta, and explained finer points therein, which were otherwise difficult to comprehend. Sri Ramakrishna preferred to tell these nuances in total privacy, when no one else would be present in the room. It was all Jnana and Yoga to begin with. Later Bhakti and Karma were added, which we shall subsequently touch upon. Sri Ramakrishna also instructed his disciples about the importance, ways, methods, and means about meditation and spiritual disciplines.[7]

Thus, between 1881 and 1886, for five years, Narendra was groomed to become a great yogi with unparalleled sharpness of intellect, reason, and spiritual knowledge. No one could stand his incisive power of critical analysis based on scientific reason and rationality in the matters of Vedanta. Added to this was the gracious gift of Sri Ramakrishna to his beloved Narendra, the gift of Nirvikalpa Samadhi -highest nondual consciousness-through which Swami Vivekananda realised the truths of super conscious states. He was face to face with Atman, the God of Sri Ramakrishna. Therefore, as is said, 'nothing else remained for Swami Vivekananda to be realised now'. He had realised the Highest Truth. But was that the case, indeed!

No. For, he still had to realise the truth of the Personal God, still had to accept that both impersonal and personal aspects of God are one and the same thing, as Shiva and Shakti are the two aspects of one Reality. God with form and God without form had relationship like that of fire and its power to burn, sun and its rays, milk and its whiteness, or diamond and its lustre. One cannot be separated from the other. On his way to the realisation of ultimate Truth, one passes through various stages, which Swami Vivekananda later elaborated in one of lectures in the USA as: 'It is like taking photographs of the sun from different locations or stations in orbit; all the photographs would appear different, but the essence of each photograph would be the same one Sun.'[8]

Karma Yoga in the Gita

The war of Kurukshretra Mahabharata became inevitable, as the last efforts to find negotiated solution by Sri Krishna also proved futile. Duryodhana was not ready for any compromises. The two armies confront each other on the battlefield where Arjuna passes through a terrible phase of remorse and melancholy - *Vishaad*. Sri Krishna tells him the Gita to allay his doubts about various paths, including Karma and worldly duties, to reach the highest Truth. What starts as a dialogue between two friends, turns into a spiritual discourse between God and a sadhaka. As if Sri Krishna was waiting for the proper opportunity to express and impart true spiritual knowledge for the welfare of the human race.

In the second chapter, Sri Krishna touches upon the Jnana Yoga (Samkhya Yoga) and Arjuna misinterprets its relevance by supposing the path of Jnana to be superior to path of Action. Thus the third Chapter begins with Arjuna putting the question: "O Keshava, if you say that Jnana is superior to Karma, then why do you insist upon me to getting involved in this ghastly and terrible war?" Will it not be better if I take to Sannyasa and lead the life as a monk?

The great bloodshed and killings of near and dear ones would thus be avoided.

Whether such feeling arose out of real pity, concern, and compassion; or whether it was the result of cowardice and fear we do not know. Sri Krishna, however, knew that such thoughts did not augur well for the progress of seekers of Truth. It was necessary to re-establish the glory of selfless work as the valid path to realisation of Atman. The impact of Jnana-based philosophy of those times was creating a wave of false adherence to Jnana. But as many sadhakas did not possess requisite qualification to undertake such sadhana of Jnana Yoga, it created an escapist trend in the social behaviour in the form of running away from the responsibilities and duties necessary for individual and collective welfare and growth.[9]

Therefore, Sri Krishna says to Arjuna, 'Your only duty is to act (right to work) and not to hanker after the fruits (or the results) thereof.' (Gita Chapter II: 47) Be not the purpose of your actions. Let not the work bind and blind you. To work is to worship; with total non-attachment and selfless attitude. Forgo all the idea of 'doership' in favour of the Lord, and with full concentration get engaged in the work at hand, i.e. the battle against the enemy. This will become Yoga for you; for 'excellence in the work is itself Yoga'.

How does excellence in work become Yoga? By preparing the mind to comprehend the essential function of Yoga i.e. to attain the purity of mind and reason through service and selflessness. To achieve excellence one must control the mind so that requisite concentration can be achieved. With practice, this control over senses and the mind reaches the degree of perfection where the spiritual aspirant (*sadhaka*) can understand the value and necessity of selfless service and renunciation to enjoy the higher state of bliss. The concentrated mind can fathom its own mysteries. Then even though the person may appear to be fully engaged in the activities he is enjoying 'the state of freedom' that his actions - spiritual disciplines - have made possible for him. Like a free bird, his mind hankers for the freedom to roam in the realm of Absolute.

Sri Krishna tells about valid actions, inaction, and improper or prohibited actions. Whatever the scriptures advocate should be accepted as correct action. Similarly, the great sages and seers, prophets and avatars also are sources for determining beneficial karma. One should follow their advice. Actions that must be shunned are those which go contrary to scriptural dictates. Such actions like hoarding, engaging in corrupt practices, bribery, doing harm to others, excessive lust, greed, hatred, jealousy, etc. make the person selfish and bind him to body-mind complex. Therefore, these are not proper karma.

The stage of inaction is quite confusing. As already mentioned, most people under the distorted pretext of Jnana become lazy and give up all good work. Their inaction falls under the category of 'tamasik inactivity' - delusory and selfish actions. Such people do not see themselves with 'inactive', but think that they are illumined and stoic Yogis. Real inaction is a gradual process of renunciation born out of the glimpses of one's True Divine nature. As a pregnant woman is gradually freed from daily routine as her term matures, and is required to concentrate on bare minimum activities essential for the timely and safe delivery, so also a sadhaka is relieved of his duties and karma to seek the Absolute. This is the state of desirable inactivity, which comes through the practice of Karma Yoga itself!

One important caveat must to be interposed here. For, as with Jnana, excessive emphasis on philanthropy is also likely to distract us from our aim of God realisation. Therefore,

Sri Ramakrishna advises us all, 'Don't go out of your way to look for such works. Undertake only those works that present themselves to you and are of pressing necessity - and those also in a spirit of detachment.' Real aim in life is realisation of God. Selfless work is difficult in this age, and at most can be a means to the end of seeking God. Sooner one is freed from the bondage of duties and responsibilities, better are the chances to seek the Divine.

While Sri Krishna was the first great person to introduce the concept of Karma Yoga, in addition to Raja, Jnana, and Bhakti, Swami Vivekananda has elaborated all the four Yogasin his lectures to western audience during his four-year stay in USA and the UK.

Swamiji's Address to World Parliament

Swami Vivekananda's spellbound speech at world parliament for religion in 1893 mesmerised the whole world. Some of the important parts of the speech are given below:

"Sisters and Brothers of America. [At this moment came the three minute standing ovation from the audience of 7,000] It fills my heart with joy unspeakable to rise in response to the warm and cordial welcome which you have given us. I thank you in name of the most ancient order of monks in the world; I thank you in the name of the mother of religions; and I thank you in the name of millions and millions of Hindu people of all classes and sects."

"My thanks also to some of the speakers on this platform who, referring to the delegates from the Orient, have told you that these men from far-off nations may well claim the honor of bearing to different lands the idea of toleration."

"I am proud to belong to a religion which has taught the world both tolerance and universal acceptance. We believe not only in universal toleration but we accept all religions as true. I am proud to belong to a nation which has sheltered the persecuted and the refugees of all religions and all nations of the earth. I am proud to tell you that we have gathered in our bosom the purest remnant of the Israelites who came to Southern India and took refuge with us in very year in which their holy temple was shattered to pieces by Roman tyranny. I am proud to belong to the religion which has sheltered and is still fostering the remnant of the grand Zoroastrian nation."

"I will quote to you brethren a few lines from a hymn which I remember to have repeated from my earliest childhood, which is every day repeated by millions of human beings: 'As the different streams having their sources in different places all mingle their water in the sea, so, O Lord, the different paths which men take through different tendencies, various though they appear, crooked or straight, all lead to Thee.'"

"The present convention, which is one of the most august assemblies ever held, is in itself a vindication, a declaration to the world of the wonderful doctrine preached in the Gita: 'Whosoever comes to me, though whatsoever form, I reach him; all men are struggling through paths which in the end lead to me.'"

"Sectarianism, bigotry, and it's horrible descendant, fanaticism, have long possessed this beautiful Earth. They have filled the earth with violence, drenched it often and often with human blood, destroyed civilisation, and sent whole nations to despair. Had it not been for these horrible demons, human society would be far more advanced than it is now."

"But their time is come; and I fervently hope that the bell that tolled this morning in honor of this convention may be the death-knell of all fanaticism, of all persecutions with the sword or with the pen, and of all uncharitable feelings between persons wending their way to the same goal".[9]

Conclusion

It was Swami Vivekananda who gave to Hinduism as a whole a clear-cut identity, a distinct profile. Before Swamiji came Hinduism was a loose confederation of many different sects. Swamiji was the first religious leader to speak about the common bases of Hinduism and the common ground of all sects. He was the first person, as guided by his Master Sri Ramakrishna, to accept all Hindu doctrines and the views of all Hindu philosophers and sects as different aspects of one total view of Reality and way of life known as Hinduism. Speaking about Swamiji's role in giving Hinduism its distinct identity, Sister Nivedita wrote: "... it may be said that when he began to speak it was of 'the religious ideas of the Hindus', but when he ended, Hinduism had been created."[10]

Before Swamiji came, there was a lot of quarrel and competition among the various sects of Hinduism. Similarly, the protagonists of different systems and schools of philosophy were claiming their views to be the only true and valid ones. By applying Sri Ramakrishna's doctrine of Harmony (Samanvaya) Swamiji brought about an overall unification of Hinduism on the basis of the principle of unity in diversity. Speaking about Swamiji's role in this field K M Pannikar, the eminent historian and diplomat, wrote: "This new Shankaracharya may well be claimed to be a unifier of Hindu ideology."

Another important service rendered by Swamiji was to raise his voice in defence of Hinduism. In fact, this was one of the main types of work he did in the West. Christian missionary propaganda had given a wrong understanding of Hinduism and India in Western minds. Swamiji had to face a lot of opposition in his attempts to defend Hinduism.

At the end of the 19th century, India in general, and Hinduism in particular, faced grave challenges from Western materialistic life, the ideas of Western free society, and the proselytising activities of Christians. Vivekananda met these challenges by integrating the best elements of Western culture in Hindu culture.

A major contribution of Vivekananda to Hinduism is the rejuvenation and modernisation of monasticism. In this new monastic ideal, followed in the Ramakrishna Order, the ancient principles of renunciation and God realisation are combined with service to God in man (Shiva jnane jiva seva). Vivekananda elevated social service to the status of divine service.

Vivekananda did not merely interpret ancient Hindu scriptures and philosophical ideas in terms of modern thought. He also added several illuminating original concepts based on his own transcendental experiences and vision of the future. This, however, needs a detailed study of Hindu philosophy which cannot be attempted here.

References

1. Vivekananda, Swami (1996). In Swami Lokeswarananda. *My India: the India eternal* (1st ed.). Calcutta: Ramakrishna Mission Institute of Culture, pp. 1-2.

2. http://www.belurmath.org/swamivivekananda.htm

3. The Complete Works of Swami Vivekananda, Volume 4.

4. Vivekananda, Swami (1996). In Swami Lokeswarananda. *My India: the India eternal* (1st ed.). Calcutta: Ramakrishna Mission Institute of Culture, pp. 1-2.

5. Vivekananda, Swami (1996). *My India: the India eternal* (1st ed.). Calcutta: Ramakrishna Mission Institute of Culture, pp. 110–111.

6. Padhy, K.S. (2011)- *Indian Political Though;* New Delhi, PHI Learning Private Limited, pp. 95-114.

7. http://www.swamij.com/swami-vivekananda-1893.htm

8. Vivekananda, Swami (1996) "*On India and Her Problems*" Advaita Ashram Publication, Almora, pp. 77-80.

9. Tejsavananda Swami (1995), "*A Short Life of Swami Vivekananda*" Kolkata Advaita Ashram Publication, pp. 106-110.

10. *Complete work of Vivekananda, Vol. III*, pp. 170-195.

6

Swami Vivekananda: Youth Icon and a Social Reformer

Deepak Yadav

12th January in India is celebrated as the National Youth day to pay tribute to the youth Icon of India Swami Vivekananda. Although Swamiji died at the tender age of just 39 years but his young age did not prevent him to gain the glory with his deep knowledge of *Vedanta*. His knowledge of *Vedas* and *Upanishads* was unparallel on which basis he countered many orthodox Hindus who were justifying untouchability, Child marriage and Sati system in the name of religion.

Swami Vivekananda was born on 12th January 1863 at Calcutta in India. His father was Vishwanath Dutta who was a successful lawyer and his mother Bhuvaneshwari Devi was a devotional and kindhearted woman. The childhood name of Swamiji was Narendra who excelled in music, gymnastic and studies by the time he graduated from Calcutta University, he had acquired the vast knowledge of different subjects especially western philosophy and history with a yogic temperament, he use to practice meditation even from his childhood, and was associated with Brahmo Movement for some time.

Before Vivekananda started his life as a monk, there were three reformat movements in India, represented by Brahmo Samaj, Arya Samaj and the Theosophical Society. But none of these movements were able to influence and inspire an average orthodox Hindu. This was the period of religious and social crisis in India, and these social movements were typing to pull in their own directions. In such a situation, the nation was in dill need of a teacher who could guide its thought, humanise its religion and its social ends and activities.[1]

On one day in November 1881, Vivekananda went to Kali Temple in Dakhshineswar where Shri Ramkrishna was staying he straightway asked the Ramakrishna; "Sir have you seen God?" without a movement's hesitation Ramkrishna replied, "Yes, I have seen him as clearly as I see you, only in a much deeper sense". Vivekananda was astonished with Ramakrisha's reply. He was also surprised to see a common simple man saying that "God can be seen". Apart from removing from doubts from the minds of Narendra, Shri Ramkrishna won him over through his pure, unselfish love. Vivekananda started visiting Dakhineswar frequently and a relationship of "Master and Disciple" developed between the two.

In 1890, Narendra get out on a long journey. He covered the length and breadth of the country. He visited Varanasi, Ayodhya, Agra, Vrindawan, Alwar, etc., Nagendra acquired the name of Swami Vivekananda during the journey. It is said that he was given the name by Maharaja of Khetri for his discrimination of things good and bad. During his journey, Vivekananda stayed at King's palaces, as well as at the huts of the poor. He came in close contract with the cultures of different regions of India and varicus classes of people in India. Vivekananda observed the imbalance and tyranny in the society in the name of caste. He realised the need for a national rejuvenation if India was to survive at all.

Swamiji considered the Vedas and Upanishads are important source of religion and culture. He tried to make a correct interpretation of the philosophy of the Upanishads through his life. He was convened that the Upanishads paved the way for the salvation presented in the Upanishads cannot be found in any literature of the world. The Upanishads restore confidence in man, they ask him to give up all weakness, pessimistique towards the life and encounter the world with strength. He also found that Upanishads preach the solidarity of this universal fraternity of man. He was inspired by the Upanishadic call to shed all ignorance, which divides men and makes them detest one another.

Vivekananda did not claim to be a philosopher or a social reformer in the traditional sense of the term. He was in fact only a religions person. According to him, much of our miseries, mutual conflicts and social evils would automatically, He said:

"*Each soul is a star, and all stars are get in that infinite arum, that eternal sky, the Lord. There is the root, the reality, the real individuality of each and all religion began with the search after some of these stars that had passed beyond out horizon, and ended in finding them all in God, and ourselves in the same place*".

Vivekananda stressed the need of religion especially at the time when the world was progressing rapidly in the field of science and technology. Although religion always worked as a great motive full, it had unfortunately, remained a basis of conflicts between the people. But different religions have the same goal. He considered variations in religions the beliefs as the sign of life and an important trait of mankind.[2]

Swamiji was orator of the religion which is rationally defined and not ingrained with dogmas. He rejected the practice of untouchability, caste oppression, Sati in Hinduism and called for the liberation of the masses. According to him:

"Each Soul is potentially Divine. The goal is to manifest this divinity within by controlling nature, external as well as internal. Do this either by work, or worship, or psychic control or philosophy - by one or more or all of there - and be free. This is the whole of religion. Doctrines of dogmas or rituals or books or temples or forms are but secondary details."

Vivekananda always treated common people and their hard lives as his source of inspiration. He said:

"There prophets were not unique, they were men as you or I. They were great Yogic. They had gained the super consciousness, and you and I can get the same. The very fact that one man ever reached that state proves that it is possible for everyman to do so. Not only it is possible, but every man must eventually, get to that state, and that is religions".[3]

Swami Vivekananda was the champion of human freedom. He said freedom is must for everyone, be it individual or a beast. It helps him to grow, prosper and realise his best-self. A society can be free only when its people one free and perfect. He further adds that man is born free but life constrained his natural freedom making him an atomised, isolated individual' who was solely interested in the unrestrained pursuit of his desires and aims which would sooner or later bring him in to conflict with the equallent freedom of another, thus cancelling each other out.

Since freedom is natural to human beings, limits to freedom would also have to be natural. Since freedom was natural to human beings, limits to freedom would have to be natural in order to retain its spontaneity. Hence, such constraints on freedom will have to come from religion. Since it could alone could develop in human beings the relationship between individuality and sociality and raise it to a sufficiently higher place of spiritual consciousness. Vivekananda felt that certain circumstances compelled man to act in a way which inhibited the freedom of others as well as went against its over will. This could not amount to a realisation of the freedom. Thus the purpose of limiting man's freedom should be refinement and not suppression. Religion defied any precise formulation and at times gave prominence to '*raj*' relegating '*Satwa*' to the background for a time.

The achievement of one's goal though freedom as well as acknowledging similar freedom for the other goes on to prove that man is essentially social, and therefore, would very much prefer living in a community. Vivekananda elucidates his thoughts with some examples. He stresses the evolution of natural communities in India as an outcome of the 'Varna' system in which 'Brahmanas' and the 'Kshatriyas' were categorised under the 'raj' 'creativity' and the 'Vaishyas' and the 'Shudras' under the 'Tam' category (instinctive desires). Such a categorisation finds similar reference in ancient Greece where Plato talked of three virtues - *Reason, Courage* and *Appetite*.

A rich source of Vivekananda's philosophy was his own experience of life. He travelled abroad extensively. Some of the truths that he preached were acquired by reflections on his own experience. Thus, his philosophy has its roots in life. One has to turn to Vivekananda's complete works to get an understanding of his philosophy. The philosophical portions of his writings are – (i) the Jnana-yoga (ii) his commentary on the abhorring of Patanjali, and (iii) the various lectures on Vedanta philosophy delivered in India and the West. His political philosophy is founded in his "Lecture from Colombo to Almora;" The East and the West; and Modern India.[4]

Roman Rolland, the French Nobel laureate in his work. "The life of Vivekananda" called Vivekananda as "the Hindu Napoleon". The Victorious marches of Vivekananda in the American continent and Europe, demonstrated to the people that Hinduism has grown powerful once more and was bent upon making spiritual, moral and cultural-philosophical propaganda in the world. The New imperialism of America and Europe met with this counterpart challenge from Asia, in the World Parliament of Religions at Chicago, in September 1833. It gave our country a new self-confidence which is the genuine psychological presagement of an independent foreign policy. Vivekananda succeeded in providing a dynamic and heroic-spiritual fernour to the formation of the culture-complex of India. Undoubtedly, his influence on some of the political teachers of Bengal life Aurbindo and Subhas Chandra Bose was intense. As a social reformer, Vivekananda always preached human equality and criticised outdated practices life untouchability, caste oppression etc. on the name of "Religion. He dedicated his life to the service of the unhappy masses. He thought of seeking material help from the West for the anticipation of conditions of the poor in exchange for the Gospel of Vedanta. He told his countrymen that there were many things which they could term from Western nations, such as their great concern for their masses, their ideal of social service, and their technique of production and economic organisation. Vivekananda was highly impressed by the material brilliance of the Western civilisation, but gradually its darker also began to be revealed to his keen vision.

As a strong believer in the philosophy of *Vedanta*, Vivekananda also found the real essence of India's religion and spirituality in the observance of Love, Service, Sacrifices and Remuneration. According to him, the religion of India which may also be called a religion of the Vedanta's, is a man-making of religion, a religion of strength and the observance of which would make any people brave, courageous and pure. No nation besoms great just by making material progress and enacting good laws. It is the strength of character of her people, which makes them great and strong. As the Vedanta wants to raise or improve the quality of men by infusing in them the strength of character, it goes to very root of the matter. That is why Vivekananda wanted to give the west the message of Vedanta in exchange for the means to improve the conditions of poors in India.

Vivekananda life mission was to open the door of spirituality to the West. He felt that religion was bound up with India's destiny. 'For good or for evil' he said that "Religions ideal has been following in India for thousands years". It has permuted the atmosphere, has entered our very blood, tinged with every drop in our veins, has become one with our constitution, has become the very vitality of our lives. Can we give it up without rousing the same energy in reaction without filling the channel which that mighty river has cut for itself in the course of millennium? Do you want that the Ganges should go back to its own bed and begins a new course? [5]

Vivekananda's visit to America and Europe developed in him a good idea of admiration for the west. The dynamism, social awareness, spirit of adventure, capacity of hard work and concern for practical values that he saw in America and Europe made a deep impression upon him. Although he saw the triumph of human spirit in the achievement of science, he also became aware of the limitation of western civilisation. In 1899, he told his Western Audience, that there was a nobler aim than accumulating wealth and conquering external nature, and that materialism could never permanently satisfy the soul of man.[6] He further told that the life" man is Atman and that the chief aim of life is to realised the divinity latent in the man. Thus, Vivekananda advised both the Indians and the Westerners. He advised Indians to learn from the West the great ideas of social service, hard labour and economic organisation, while his message to the Western friends was to follow the spiritual truth of India contained in the *Vedanta*.

Swami Vivekananda's concepts on religion, education, social service, nationalism, upliftment of downtrodden, dignity of labour classes, emancipation of women were all noble ideas which in turn inspired India's freedom movement. It is said that he inspired Jamshed ji Tata to set up India Institute of sciences. He countered the propaganda spread by the colonial state and the Christian missionaries about Hinduism being an observant, idolatrous, and backward and casteist religion. Swamiji, teachings included sense of unity, pride in the part and sense of mission - the futons which gave real strength and purpose to India's nationalist movement. Indians have gained unprecedented self-respect, self-reliance and self-assertion from his teachings.

Swamiji's unique contribution to the creation of new India was to open the minds of his fellow countrymen to their duty towards the poor and depressed classes. Long before the Marxist ideology was known in India, Swamiji spoke about the role of toiling masses in the production of national wealth. Swamiji was a religious leader in India who spoke for the masses, formulated a definite philosophy of service and organised large scale socio-religious institutions to serve the poor and depressed. He said, "Do not forget that the downtrodden, the ignorant, the poor, the unlettered, the cobblers, the sweepers are your flesh and blood, your relations.[7] Swamiji's nationalism was based on his deep love for his motherland and also on his philosophy of Advaita Vedanta. Swamiji was very sympathetic towards downtrodden and oppressed classes of society. He therefore felt more poignantly the murderous inequality of the castes and the outcasts of India, He said,

"*India's doom was sealed the very day they invented the word. Malechchha (the none Hindu, the man outside) and stopped from communion with other.*" He preached the primordial necessity of an organisation that will teach Hindus mutual help and appreciation after the pattern of Western democracies.

Swamiji demanded complete equality for all. He said, "Let every woman, man and child without respect of caste or birth, weakness of strength, hear and learn that behind the strong and the weak, behind the high and low, behind everyone, there is that infinite soul of all become great and good. Let us proclaim to every soul Arise, awake! Awake from this hypnotism of weakness."

He further added that, "*If the Brahmana has more aptitude for learning on the ground of heredity than the pariah, spend no more money on the Brahmana's education, but spend all on the Pariah. Give the weak, for there all the gifts is needed. If the Brahmin is born cleaver, he can educate himself without help.... This is justice and reason as I understand it.*"[8]

Conclusion

The life of Swami Vivekananda itself was the message to the world. While protecting the basic tenets of Hinduism, he always encouraged people to accept the scientific temper of the west. He criticised the priestly class who are sticking with the religions scriptures while practicing outdated religions practices.

He tried to remedy social injustices by proceeding intermarriage between the castes and sub-divisions of casts near to each-other, by ameliorating the conditions of out castes, by occupying himself with the fate of unmarried women and of Hindu widows, by righting sectarianism whenever it was to be found, and vain formalism the "do not touchism" as he called them.

Swamiji always preached for communal harmony and treated all religions equal. The guiding principles of Hinduism was to never attack anybody's faith, to present the doctrine of Vedas in the simplest form so that it might be accessible to all, to find room for definite questions of hygiene and education, and physical and educational betterment of race, and to spread ideas of moral purity, mutual aid, and universal harmony.

With Vivekananda started the discovery of India and her journey in a fast emerging new world. His appearance at the plateform of the Parliament of Religions in America in 1893 was an event that shook the whole west with his personality and message of human unity through - Advaita which attracted the scholars like Max Mueller, Paul Deussen and a little later writers and thinkers like Romaine Rolland. In true sense, Swamiji was a universal man with universal values.

References

1. Das and Patro (1988), "*Indian Political Traditions*", New Delhi, Sterling Publishes, pp. 79-95.
2. *Ibid.*, pp. 79-95.

3. *The Life of Vivekananda,* Vol. II, pp. 270–77.
4. Das and Patro - op.cit. - pp. 80–81.
5. Basu, Sankari, "*Swami Vivekananda in contemporary Indian News - 1893–1902*", Ramkrishna Mission Institute of Culture, Calcutta, 1997, pp. 150–155.
6. Basu Shasmita, "*Religious Revivalism and Nationalist Discourse: Swami Vivekananda and New Humanism in 19th Century Bengal.*" Oxford University Press, Delhi 2002, p. 213.
7. Vivekananda Swami, "*Bartaman Bharat,*" Udbodhan Publisher, Culcutta, 1962, pp. 34-36.
8. Rolland Romain, "A *Colossus Named Vivekananda Whose Mission Awaits Complition*", Farsight Publishers, Delhi, 2010, pp. 144-145.

7

Vivekananda's Political Ideas

Nivedita Giri

'ivekananda said in 1894, "Let no political significance be ver attached falsely to any of my writings or sayings. What onsense! I do not believe in politics. God and Truth are the nly policies in the world, everything else is trash."[1] But, owever, today, Vivekananda's sayings related to politics eem to be very appropriate for a good political system.

Vivekananda, a seeker of the truth from his childhood, ad an exceptional mind-set. While wondering setting up a niversal, ideal principle which could cleanse the society or inds of people at grassroots level he met Sri Ramakrishna aramahansa, who was involved in the discourse on Hindu ıd other religions. Sri Ramakrishna's liberalistic approach, ho had no institutional academic background, attracted arendra (Swami Vivekananda). Narendra reformed into vami Vivekananda took the vow of preaching this great ıilosophical wisdom to the world torn in war and struction. He pointed out that, neglect and exploitation of e poor was one of the main causes of India's downfall and ckwardness. He said, "so long as the millions lives in hunger and ignorance, I hold every man a traitor who having been educated at their expense, pays not the least heed to them"[2], has inspired many young people to take up social service as a way of life.

Swami Vivekananda has symbolized himself as a leading spiritual leader and philosopher, a true guide and a devoted friend of not only the Indian people but also the whole world. He was one of the chief architects of Indian renaissance. He awakened the country's masses from the slumber of self-degradation and stimulated their sense about its cultural and national glory. He enlightened the global civilization about their responsibilities towards mankind. His writings and speeches were a source of inspiration for many political leaders of Indian freedom struggle like Netaji Subhas Chandra Bose, Mahatma Gandhi, Jawaharlal Nehru, Rajagopalachari and many more. Besides, the philosophical foundation Vivekananda's political thought has also influenced greatly towards the nation building. His beliefs in secularism, universal brotherhood, nationalism, socialism, ethnicity, multiculturalism, and development are greater relevance to our political system today. This section tries to deal with these thoughts of Vivekananda in some details.

Secularism

With his own concept of Vedanta, Vivekananda gave the country the secularist ideal that now forms a part of Indian Constitution. He was first to proclaim on world platform that all religions show different paths that led to the same goal. His idea of secularism was, in fact, an advance of what is found in modern India. He wanted not just mutual tolerance but mutual respect and, what is more, mutual recognition of the basic truth that underlies all religions.

Swamiji did not hesitate to speak his mind about any religion. While he believed that Advaita Vedanta 'is the future of enlightened humanity, he persuaded that without the help of practical Islam, theories of Vedantaism, however fine they may be, are entirely valueless to mankind'. Therefore, "I see in my mind's eye the future-perfect India rising out of this chaos and strife, glorious and invincible, with Vendanta brain and Islam body."[3] Ultimately, "we want to lead mankind to the place where there is no Vedas, Bibles or Koran.Yet this has to be done by harmonizing the Vedas, the Bible and the Koran. Mankind ought to be taught that religions are but the varied expressions of the Religion, which is oneness, so that each may choose the path that suits him best."[4]

Vivekananda once said that sectarianism, bigotry and its horrible descendant, fanaticism, have filled the world with violence, drenched it often with human blood and destroyed civilization. His Hinduism was "a religion which has taught the world both tolerance and universal acceptance".

India takes pride in being secular now, but generations of Indians are growing up knowing very little about what it is that makes Hinduism or Sanatan Dharma, which is so accepting of other religions. The Indians need to understand that our worldview makes us all-inclusive to fight against any kind of fundamentalism.

Vivekananda's understanding of Vedanta made him a total opponent to the practice of untouchability in Indian society. Denouncing, as he did, the practice of untouchability, Vivekananda anticipated, by several decades, the more effective campaign that Gandhi and Ambedkar carried on against this social evil. He found neither religious sanction nor secular logic behind the terrible practice of untouchability and he went all out to condemn it.

Universal Brotherhood

In 1893 Swami Vivekananda arrived in Chicago as a protagonist of Hinduism to present his case before the

Parliament of Religion. He carried the Vedantic message of solidarity of mankind as particles of God. It was in fact his Universal humanism based on what he called 'practical Vedanta'. He propagated and taught us the universal oneness based on Advaita.

Vivekananda gave a message of the unity of all humanity. He said, "If you go below the surface, you find that unity between man and man, between races and races, high and low, rich and poor, gods and men and men and animals. If you go deep enough, all will be seen as only variation of the One; and he who has attained to this conception of Oneness has no more delusion".[5]

The spirit of universal love and brotherhood was what impelled Vivekananda to establish in 1897 a new monastic order, whose remit was activities for "the establishment of fellowship among followers of various religions, knowing them all to be so many forms of only one undying eternal religion."[6]

Nationalism

The history of Vivekananda's life is correlated with the awakening of India and the resuscitation of Indian religion. But how much agony and suffering that mighty soul had to undergo before he was able to set in motion machinery which was to bring about an all-round awakening in Indian national life. The influence of Vivekananda on the nationalist India is well-known. It was Vivekananda who first spoke of a revolution in India to be led by *Sudras*. We all know that this great soul of India belonged to a monastic order. He was never tired of stressing the need to revive the ancient glory of our country. But alongside this he was emphatic in his speeches and writings on the need to awaken our masses for a revolution that would bring about sweeping changes in our bodypolitic and build for India an entirely new cultural pattern and way of life.

The twenty-first century liberal ideas and humanistic outlook found their logical culmination in Vivekananda's strident call for this revolution to be brought about by the masses kept in social and economic bondage through centuries. He was a revolutionary all through his life and one of the pioneers of socialist movement in India. Liberal in his views, he was opposed to all kinds of superstitions and bigotry. This had a salutary effect on his thinking. While in childhood he came under the influence of the Brahmo movement and this helped him a great deal in rising above all pettiness born of casteism and superstitions. He came to develop a rational approach to life and its problems.

Vivekananda was a true nationalist to the core and believed in patriotism and national feeling. He was proud of the Indian legacy with the cultural approach and he was of the view that every nation is born and not created. According to him, "Every nation has a national purpose of its own. Either in obedience to the law of nature, or by virtue of the superior genius of the great ones, the social manners and customs of every nation are molded into shape, so as to bring that purpose with fruition."[7] Vivekananda wanted each nation should to grow to its full stature and strength, thus contributing to the sum total of world's growth and human welfare. Vivekananda's nationalism had internationalism in essence and execution.

Universally acclaimed as a pioneer in the field of national liberation in India, Swami Vivekananda was complex personality being a lover of humanity, a world teacher of religion, a great patriot, and a leader of the Indian people. Truly he has been regarded as a patriot-saint of modern India and an inspirer of her dormant consciousness, who instilled a freshness and vigour into it.

According to C. P. Ramaswami Aiyar, Swami Vivekananda was a democratic saint. He revived for us the idea of nationhood. He was the first of those, who made it possible to think of India as a whole irrespective of the existing differences of class, creed, colour and custom. He pleaded for the driving away of everything that would prevent the union of India. He knew that unless India was one spiritually and intellectually, India could not step into the outer world. A distracted, quarrelsome, feeble minded India would not be of any assistance in the world and therefore he said, Unite ... our ship of religion and of State is now laden full of many cargos, precious, some by no means precious, some wholly nugatory. We must throw aside such cargo. The storm is there. The great winds are blowing and unless the useless cargo is thrown aside, the ship will sink. Swami asked us to sink the unnecessary cargo. And unless we got that lesson India will perish as the several other nations have perished. ...His gospel was the gospel of courage, of hope and admiration, of eschewal and assimilation.

Socialism

Swami Vivekananda redefined our outlook to human nature and society. Swamiji's masterful oratory was a source of optimism and inspiration for the advance of human prosperity and emancipation. He was totally committed to the cause of the oppressed and was ready to sacrifice everything for that cause. He was a revolutionary thinker who pioneered a radical change, in his own unique way.

Swami Vivekananda once said, "I do on believe in a God or Religion that does not bring a piece of bread to the orphan's mouth or wipe away the widow's tears."[8] Such strong statement reflects his constant concern for the common people and his vision of a religion that is practical and provides the individual with the inspiration to know and seek God.It also shows the socialist side of his nature. Swami Vivekananda was deeply disturbed by the inequities that prevailed in Indian society. He wished that there should be equality in the society. He just could not accept the fact that the gap between the rich and the poor was something that could not be bridged. India of today is not very different from what it was then. Today the top 20 per cent of Indians generate and control 85 per cent of India's wealth, while the bottom 20 per cent for whom Swamiji's heart bleed, generate and control a mere 1.5 per cent of India's wealth.

Swami Vivekananda believed in raising the poor and ignorant masses not through mere doles, but wanted them to be empowered and made capable of building their own destinies and making them self-reliant. He wanted that the 'haves', the affluent in the society to play greater role to create an enabling and facilitatory environment, wherein the poor could raise themselves up without affecting their self-esteem and dignity. This thought was later endorsed by Mahatma Gandhi in his believe in trusteeship. He was not only sensitive to the economic disparities but was deeply pained by the social inequities that were prevailing. He considered that the great national sin was the neglect of the masses and that was one of the causes of India's downfall. He wanted these masses to be well-educated, well fed and well cared for. He said, "If you want to regenerate India, we must work for them."[9] For him growth of the nation lies on the rise of the poor.

For Swamiji, bringing in equity was not by bringing down the rich but by pushing up the poor. This is so very relevant in today's India. We now have a country wherein more than 200 districts are affected by violence, and people are adopting the ideology of bringing in social equity from the barrel of a gun which is understood as Naxalism. 'Evolution' should be the path for social rising up in India not 'revolution', Swamiji often remarked. This was a great foresight he had.

Vivekananda understood that people would not sit and tolerate inequity for too long. They would get restless and take to addressing this problem from an emotive plane rather than from a rational one. An agitated and restless group of people can be easily motivated to take to violence with disastrous consequences. At the same time, Swamiji also understood that a country could not truly grow and thrive till the benefits of economic prosperity reached out to the last man on the street. He also understood that mere charity can be very demeaning and take away human enterprise and initiative. This would also not be a sustainable and permanent way of solving this problem. He urged people to see religion as a means of serving the less fortunate without snatching away their sense of pride, dignity and self-esteem. He wanted this kind of assistance to be life-giving and enabling. He wanted to make sure that the masses would once and for all be raised and would not have to depend either on a benevolent government or on a philanthropic society. This practical and non-violent way-forward would neither create insecurity in the minds of the wealthy nor any negative emotion in the people trying to climb up the economic ladder.

As a man of religion and meditation, Vivekananda was all for activity that would lead to increase in production and the removal of poverty. He always said that, "religion is not for empty stomachs." He shocked people out of their self-complacency and plunged them into action. Thus, he influenced the course of life in modern India by stimulating the Rajasic qualities in the Indian people, and getting them to set about the task of betterment of their material conditions of life rather than get lost in a soporific religion that produced contentment with their existing life of poverty and degradation. In Vivekananda's opinion, religion had to be the principal and leading force in implementing all social changes in India.

Swamiji's attitude towards socialism is summed up in, "I am a socialist, not because it is a perfect system, but because I believe that half a loaf is better than no bread."[10] Swamiji saw socialism as a ray of hope for the myriad of problems confronting India. He viewed the course of world history as a change in governance between the four castes—Brahmin, Kshatriya, Vaishya and Shudra in conformity to the law of nature. With the rise of Shudras, the lowest class, Vivekananda identified democracy and distribution of physical comforts and education. Swamiji's concept of socialism was in no way averse to religion. He believed in elevation of masses without injuring the religious sentiments and that social changes can be brought forward only on a firm platform of conduct character and spirituality.

No doubt, Vivekananda took pride in the country's inheritance from the past, but he was not a scholar revivalist with undiscriminating admiration for all that had come down from the past. To him, India meant the people and the people meant the masses. Removal of poverty, eradication of illiteracy, restoration of human dignity, freedom from fear, availability of spiritual and secular knowledge to all, irrespective of their caste and class and the ending of all monopolies, religious, economic, intellectual, social and cultural - all these formed a part of what he derived from his practical Vedanta or Vedantic socialism.

Through his re-interpretation of Vedanta, and his deep concern for the masses and their problems, Vivekananda gave the country a new lease of life. Raising his voice against colonial and feudal oppression, Vivekananda searched, at the same time, for an answer to the question of India's historical destinies, of the ways and means of transforming it into a wealthy, strong and independent state. He insistently repeated that India could be roused and rebuilt with the help of small groups of enthusiastic patriots, strong and courageous with "muscles of iron and nerves of steel and gigantic wills".

Vivekananda's Vedantic socialism is also reflected in his endeavour to give India's traditional religions a new orientation of social service. By establishing the Ramakrishna Mission, he gave an altogether new direction to the role of monks in Indian society. As a result, for the first time in Indian history, we have the Hindu monks who do not isolate themselves from society, but actively concern themselves with its service and betterment. They have set up educational institutions, hospitals, dispensaries, orphanages and other social institutions for alleviating human suffering. They are also in the forefront in the work of relief and rehabilitation whenever the country suffers from natural disasters such as droughts, floods, cyclones and epidemics.

Development

Swami Vivekananda's thoughts for development of a country are followed at present by national leaders as well as leaders of other countries. He was supporter of inclusive growth. In the globalised world when India is fighting against several odds for achieving growth in all sectors what India needs today are leaders and planners who can think and act like Vivekananda for sustainable development of the nation. Otherwise, the rapid growth that we see today will continue to rest in the hands of a chosen few. And this could only strengthen the hands of those who ideologically believe that a violent snatching away from the rich is the only way to provide for the poor.

It is clear that India needs a very different approach to development instead of few government schemes. It is the need of the hour that India creates systems that further human capital through education and vocations infused with the sense of human and personal dignity would be one step towards sustainable development. Another important march towards development of the common people is to create an environment with ample opportunities accessible to all without any discrimination on the basis of caste, creed, race and religion.

Institutionalization of such principles in developmental initiatives not only has social and moral responsibility, but also has a strong business sense in any country.

Expanding the pool of human resources that are productively engaged enhances national productivity leading to prosperity. Indian including other developing nations must address the issues of poverty and other challenges among its most neglected people for their holistic growth. The simplistic view of only meeting immediate needs of food, water, and shelter are no longer sustainable. Therefore, the governments and civil societies must work hard to ensure restoring human dignity and sense of self-worth among the 'have nots' and instill faith in human enterprise and in our ability to change our circumstances without relying on others.

Trained economists may take years to frame some idea about the problems faced by the country and its people and then suggest measures to solve them. But it was the brilliance of Swami Vivekananda who could not only understand the problems of the people but also suggested such measures which are of extreme relevance even today. He was concerned about agriculture and its improvement and wanted to educate the farmers as well as to modernize it by using new technology. He talks of industrialization of the country at the same time he pleads for the continuance of small scale and cottage industry. He talks of trade with countries but not aid will enhance economic growth. This was raised by the third world countries during sixties where as Vivekananda spoke about it decades ago. He suggests complete programme of poverty eradication based on Vedantic philosophy. It is true that, the strategy and programmes of our national life would not be properly adopted without the analysis of Swami Vivekananda. Our modern and developing national life is very sounded by the thought of Swami Vivekananda. During establishing the democracy in India, it is 'Development' that the basic aim that had adopted by our national leaders. Although this 'development' does not refer only the 'physical development', but it is also the development of mass consciousness, national integration, and social welfare, those had referred to be practiced in our national life.

Vivekanand believed that the development of villages would be accelerated only if educated men went to live in the villages ensuring "that which is necessary for our nation will be achieved."[11] He viewed, a sort of brotherly feeling between the higher and the lower castes should be in the society." The Indian political leaders these days must take lesson from this saying who practice caste-politics and divide the society that leads to destruction only instead of any development.

Ethnicity

From teachings of Swami Vivekanand, one can easily understand that, how much ethnic pride Swamiji had. He was a great propagator of Indian culture, history, food and languages. This can be more analysed as Annie Besant writes, in the Parliament of Religions, Vivekananda's figure was instinct with pride of country, pride of race–the representative of the oldest of living religions, surrounded by curious gazers of nearly the youngest religions. India was not to be shamed before the hurrying arrogant West by this her envoy and her son. He brought her message, he spoke in her name, and the herald remembered the dignity of the royal land whence he came. Purposeful, virile, strong, he stood out, a man among men, able to hold his own. On the platform another side also came out. The dignity and the inborn sense of worth and power still were there, but all was subdued to the exquisite beauty of the spiritual message which he had brought, to the sublimity of that matchless truth of the East which is the heart and the life of India, the wondrous teaching of 'the Self'.

Vivekananda Today

After sixty-six years of independence, India is still in the twilight zone of political turmoil, economic imbalance, social turbulence and ideological confusion. Though we claim to be the largest democracy in the world, more often than not our democracy in practice turns out to be acrimonious monocracy. Economically, statistics are trotted out to prove that we made enviable progress. But, in effect, the divide between the rich and the poor has increased enormously. Society is fast disintegrating into organized caste and communal groups reducing nationalism to a meaningless slogan. All the universities together along with various other specialized educational and training institutions have produced possibly the largest contingent of intelligentsia in the world but in terms of awareness and enlightenment about our country, its history, its culture and its due role in the international arena, they are a confused and directionless lot. Consequently, we as a nation have not been able to play our part in the national and international affairs despite our invaluable culture, enormous population and immense and diverse natural resources.

What is most unfortunate is that, there has been a rapid decline in the moral and ethical values both at the individual and collective levels. For a country whose unique strength is rooted in spirituality which is the basis of all values, this is a fatal lapse which undermines the very rationale of our existence. Before we could settle down as a stable and vibrant socio-economic and political power, globalization at a furious pace has engulfed us with its enormous demands and pressures. Our political leadership at the helm of affairs has proved unequal to the task of leading the nation into its rightful place among the comity of nations.

This is in sharp contrast with the unshakable confidence, the tremendous will power and the clarity of vision which were our assets during our freedom struggle. Unless this widening gulf is bridged and we regain the national self-confidence and the glorious sense of mission, the confusion cannot be cleared and the sense of direction retrieved. These unhappy thoughts stare us on the face with deep poignancy as we celebrate another birth anniversary of Swami Vivekananda, whose life and mission were the inspiration for almost all our stalwarts of the freedom movement. It will not be far from truth to say that all the subsequent failures, clashes and conflicts, doubts and dilemmas are directly traceable to that one major failure to follow Swamiji's exhortation. Dedication to the Motherland, which is the sheet anchor of patriotism - the highest value which all our freedom fighters cherished, was abandoned and along with that every other value became negotiable. Cheerful and robust optimism gave way to sterile cynicism.

During this period, the world has changed a lot. India is no exception. New ideas and ideologies have swept across the country, most of them foreign. The stirring words and the glowing example of Swami Vivekananda, who can rightly be called the 'Mantra Drashta' of Modern India, have increasingly been marginalized from our mainstream thought currents while nothing else could even be thought of as a fairly viable substitute. There is all-around selfishness, corruption, power politics, communal conflicts etc. No wonder, at one point of time, Indian leadership could not help thinking of restoring Swamiji to the center stage by declaring his birthday as 'National Youth Day'. Like every other government order, the celebration of Swamiji's birthday as the "National youth day" became a secular ritual devoid of its spiritual and patriotic content.

Swamiji was a staunch nationalist. He spoke passionately about our nation and its greatness. He imparted to us a profound vision of our role in forging a new world order. But with the present craze for globalization, our youth find it difficult even to accept the concept of Nation. National pride appears to them anachronistic, in the rapidly changing world situation. The vision of India's role is now confined to certain areas of technological innovations and professional expertise. There is no philosophy of patriotism to guide them and hence there is no depth in their approach. At present they are citizens of a world dominated by momentary and throw away everything including inviolable family ties—culture. India is the land with the largest and brightest population of promising youths. But, how to equip and inspire them with a sense of mission, a true spirit of conviction and unreserved commitment for the sake of a noble ideal, how to clear the confusion that clouds their vision. It is precisely here that, Swami Vivekananda becomes really relevant.

Swamiji has given us a perfectly tenable, logical and comprehensive answer to all the doubts and questions that the present situation has thrown up. Globalization or internationalism does not invalidate nationalism, says Swamiji. In fact, without nationalism there can be no internationalism. Internationalism, ideally, is the happy and peaceful co-existence of all the nations, big or small. Nationalism is an essential stage of human evolution which cannot be abolished for any foreseeable future. Therefore, from the very start, we must have to understand the mission of our own race, the destiny it has to fulfill, the place it has to occupy in the march of nations, the note which it has to contribute to the harmony of races. The fulfillment of that mission is the purpose of its existence. This is true of every nation and each one is naturally expected to cooperate and coordinate with other nations. All together constitute the harmonious human family. That was the ancient Hindu concept of

'Vasudhaiva Kutumbakam'. Coordination among and not domination over other nations is the ideal.

To the superficial observers, globalization is going to be the final word in man's civilization march. It is sometimes believed that the whole world and all countries and cultures are going to be steam rolled into one homogeneous totality. But history tells us that this cannot be. Human nature is so complex that it will not accept homogeneity as its ideal. All such attempts have failed miserably. Imperialism, Communism, Socialism, etc have shared the same fate of temporary success and ultimate collapse. There was a time when it was claimed that the "Sun will never set on the British Empire."[12] Communism during its hey days proclaimed that it is going to bring the whole humanity under its red banner. Swamiji's prediction that no social philosophy or social order, however, lofty or noble, can sustain itself unless it has the Vedantic philosophy of Advaita as its foundation. That is how socialism and Communism have collapsed, in spite of their objective of equality and social justice. Globalization is another milestone which will also be over passed. It will leave its imprint, no doubt, but only like earlier civilization phases. One thing is clear. Whether it is Imperialism or Communism, Socialism or Globalism, none of these can overturn or nullify nationalism. That will remain the corner stone for the future human civilization. It will ensure human unity with cultural diversity which is nature's or call it God's - Design! What is India's role in all these? Swami Vivekananda stated unambiguously that, India's soul lies in its spirituality and its world mission is to evolve spiritually and help humanity with its spiritual — Vedantic ideals. But Swamiji hastened to assure that spirituality does not mean either a cluster of rituals or mere other worldliness. Spirituality is a way of life here and now, it includes 'Sarnutkarsha and Nishreyasa' — material development and spiritual enlightenment. He envisaged future India as a spiritually enlightened nation, firmly standing as an economically prosperous, socially harmonious and technologically well-equipped, national foundation in total harmony with the rest of the world.

Swamiji believed that India has a dual role to play, one imparting spirituality to the materially advanced countries of the West while learning from them the techniques of organization, and second mutual cooperation and technological advancement' in order to make India's development balanced and total. India should go to the West, he said, as a teacher, as a Guru and not as a begger with a begging bowl. That will bring us respect. Swamiji himself was a shining example. We must uncompromisingly adhere to our cultural way of life. We may accept and assimilate certain useful ideas from others, and still be ourselves in all essentials. In his famous Chicago speech he proclaimed why the whole world needs India's unique teaching. There are lessons which the world needs which India alone can teach. They are more relevant today than they were at the time he delivered the historical message. Making a special reference to the Parliament of Religion he said, the present convention, which is one of the most august assemblies ever held, is in itself a vindication, a declaration to the world, of the wonderful doctrine preached in the Gita, Whosoever comes to Me, through whatever form, I reach him; all men are struggling through paths which in the end lead to Me. Sectarianism, bigotry, and its horrible descendant, fanaticism, have long possessed this beautiful earth. They have filled the earth with violence, drenched it often and often with human blood, destroyed civilization, and sent whole nations to despair. Had it not been for these horrible demons, human society would be far more advanced than it is now. But, their time is gone, and I fervently hope that the bell that tolled this morning in honour of this convention may be the death knell of all fanaticism, of all persecutions wither the sword or with the pen, and of all uncharitable feelings between persons wending their way to the same goal. There is no room for religious conflicts or intolerance, much less for the haunting specter of terrorism. Swamiji's words were prophetic and its relevance continues with greater urgency.

A great disservice has been done to Swami Vivekananda by the post independence intellectuals of India by creating the impression that to call oneself a Hindu is something to be ashamed about. There had been a systematic campaign at the highest levels to propagate that the Swamiji was not in favor of calling India a Hindu nation. The implication was that the Hindu was a narrow and communal nomenclature and as such the name is better kept out of vogue. Coming as it did from very high and respectable quarters this propaganda made deep impact. It was a very calculated and dishonest attempt to pit Swami Vivekananda against whatever was Hindu in name and content. There was an ideological underpinning to the vicious propaganda with a deep political motivation. It was the objective of the "leftist, secular and so called progressive"[13] intelligentsia to destroy the genuine cultural nationalism of our country and to tear apart the fabric of our national unity. By this clever ploy, backed by the ruling elite, they succeeded to a large extent in weakening the pride in Hindu nationalism. In fact, this was totally against Swamiji's perception.

Swamiji was one of the first and foremost exponents of Hindu Nationalism. Even at that time there were people, among them some sections of Hindus, who considered Hindu a bad word having notorious connotation. Swamiji had openly declared that he was one of the proudest of Hindus. Great people like Mahayogi Sri Aurobindo, following the footsteps of Swami Vivekananda were fully convinced that ours is a Hindu nation and Sanatana Dharma was its very soul.

Sanatana Dharma and Hindu Dharma had identical connotations, according to them. He had consistently used the term Hindu nationalism in his lectures and writings. Even his definition of nationalism that "National union in India must be a gathering up of its scattered spiritual forces. A Nation in India must be a union of those whose hearts beat to the same spiritual tune"[14] makes it clear. Needless to say, it had nothing negative or reactionary about it. But, unfortunately, politically biased propaganda against the word has resulted in weakening the nation's pride in its history, culture, tradition and worldview. This has done immense harm to the noble cause which Swamiji held in high esteem and wakened our national integrity and identity. The modern educated intelligentsia began to internalize the demeaning idea that they are a rootless people who were never a nation and thus fell victims to the false propaganda that India is only a "Nation in the making". This is one of the major reasons for the moral and cultural decline in post-independence India. Swamiji's birthday is an occasion for the Hindus to initiate a legitimate self-assertion.

Swami Vivekananda would have gladly welcomed the beneficial aspects of Globalization to the best advantage of India and the rest of the world, as it could provide India with abundant channels of communication to transmit the treasures of spiritual wisdom to the western world which is deeply engrossed in mindless materialism and vulgar consumerism. In many of his lectures he has reminded us as to how this has happened many a time in the past. Whenever nations of the world have been brought closer together by imperial adventurers or religious missionaries or trading companies, Swamiji has pointed out that, India had made use of such occasions for pouring out her spiritual and cultural blessings to the world at large. Such an ideal situation has presented itself today. As a natural consequence, India's spiritual message is, no doubt, reaching out into all corners of the world, slowly but steadily, creating its firm and positive impact. But a more self-confident and assertive India could have contributed much more effectively and successfully and could have influenced the trend of global policies in a more specific manner. But, it is an unfortunate fact that, while the world is prepared and even eager to embrace India for her rich gift of spirituality and our spiritual leaders are making their appeal in their own way, the official India appears to be fighting shy of publicly owning up our innate spiritual and cultural identity. A totally misconceived concept of secular politics seems to be compelling them to adopt a hypocritical stand of distancing themselves from this unique legacy.

Globalisation has brought about another dimension in the East-West relationships. They represent two different kinds of civilisations. Swamiji had stated in one of his lectures that the West created a model of civilisation that measured its success in terms of how much a man can possess and how much one can enjoy. The Eastern civilization measured its success in terms of how little a man needs to possess and still happily live. America represented the Western civilisation and India the Eastern. The Indian civilisation centered round the concept of "Aparigraha" or non-acquisition and renunciation, where as the Western had "Upabhoga" meaning consumerism as its fulcrum. In puranic terminology, it would be said that the East and West had the 'Dadheechi' and 'Yayathi' syndromes respectively. In the globalised society, East and West have closely come together into a global village forget for the moment with the fiercely competitive global market, in which these two types come into conflict, yet have to coexist. It is clear that India has to play a vital role to impart its unique culture of 'Aparigraha' to temper the consumeristic mania of the West and enable the world to strike a healthy balance.

Another aspect, which Swamiji has pointed out is that, the Hindu civilisation has no problem with the modern science. He said, the Hindu is only glad that what he has been cherishing in his bosom for ages is going to be taught in iron forcible language, and with further light from the latest conclusions of science. But it is not so easy for other religion to accept the findings of science and still be believers in the tenets of their religion. As Swami Ranganathananda puts it, "But in the West the Christian theology never allowed science to proceed deeper and deeper. They tried to stop it and even killed a few scientists. So, a few well-tested truths of science could demolish the whole dogmas of Christian religion in the modern West." Indian spirituality and modern science will fulfill each other and lay down the foundation for the future civilisation of mankind.

Summing Up

In conclusion, a thought provoking statement by the world renowned historian A. L Basham regarding Swamiji must be noted here, "Even now, a hundred years after the birth of Narendranath Dutta, who later became Swami Vivekananda, it is very difficult to evaluate his importance in the scale of world's history. It is certainly far greater than any Western historian or most Indian historians would have suggested at the time of his death. The passing of years and the many stupendous and unexpected events which have occurred since then suggest that in centuries to come he will be remembered as one of the main moulders of the modern world".

In Swamiji, we find a complete reformer who knew the philosophy, economics, politics, society, cultures, religion and everything related to human life. In Hinduism, the ultimate aim of human life is the attainment of salvation or Moksha. To attain Moksha, a conducive socio-economic order wherein an individual can lead a peaceful and undistracted life is imperative. Marxism also professes the attainment of a different order, that is, a classless society. A socialist state has no exploitation and the individual is freed from the burden of having to work for those who exploit his labour whereby leading to a classless society.Though not in politics, Vivekananda did exert a visible influence on the political development and on the modern India that has emerged from this development. In a sense, he was politically far ahead of his time in the importance he attached to the masses, the indignation he displayed on their exploitation, the genuine concern he had for the uplift of women and the backward classes and, above all, in his strong desire for the country to get the benefit of Western science and technology for its development without falling into the trap of slavish imitation of the Western ways of life. The revolutionary ideas he propounded had a tremendous influence on subsequent political thinking and action in India, especially on the mass-dynamism of Mahatma Gandhi and the socialistic ideas of Jawaharlal Nehru.

Vivekananda was not against reforms, but he believed that India needed radical reforms. In his book, 'On India and Her Problems', he wrote, "Remember that the nation lives in the cottages. But, alas, nobody ever did anything for them. Our modern reformers are very busy about widow-remarriage. Of course, I am a sympathiser in every reform, but the fate of a nation does not depend upon the number of husbands the widows get, but upon the condition of the masses". Vivekananda went a step further and said, "So long as millions live in hunger and ignorance, I hold every man a traitor." He sincerely believed that the only hope of India was from the masses, for the upper classes were physically and morally dead. He believed that, a time would come when the masses would rise, throw off the dominance of the upper classes and establish their absolute supremacy.

With his reinterpretation of Vedanta, Swami Vivekananda played a key role in the shaping of modern India. Socialism, secularism, mass upliftment and mass power, abolition of untouchability, universal literacy, informal education, women's liberation and inculcation of social service, as a part of religious worship these constituted the quintessence of his "Vedantic socialism". His sociological views played a positive role in the development of the patriotic and national self-consciousness of the youth of India. Vivekananda's clamant call to the Indian youth, "Awake, arise, and stop not till the goal is reached," is resounding all through India, rousing their social consciousness and kindling their damp spirits.

References

1. The Complete Works of Swami Vivekananda, Volume 5.
2. Swami Vivekananda, Life and Teachings.
3. The Complete Works of Swami Vivekananda, Volume 6.
4. The Week, Anniversary Special, Vol. No. 53, December 30, 2012, Mumbai.
5. Manoj Sadasivan, Religion Vs Socialism, A Comparative Study of Vivekananda and Marx.
6. Swami Vivekananda, Life and Teachings.
7. Vivekananda - The Revolutionary Swami, Mainstream Weekly, 2010, New Delhi.
8. The Complete Works of Swami Vivekananda; Volume 6.
9. Meditation on Divine Unity - Fourth Dimension Inc., Sri Ramkrishna Seva Kendra - Tolani.Org.
10. Bridging Economic Inequity, The Vivekananda Way, Balu's Musings, June 11, 2012.
11. Swami Adiswarananda, *Vivekananda, World Teacher*: His Teachings on The Spiritual Unity, 2006.
12. Narasingha Prosad Sil, Swami Vivekananda: A Reassessment, Associate University Presses, Cranbury, 1997.
13. Gautam Ghosh, A *Biography of Swami Vivekananda*, Rupa & Co., 2003.
14. The Complete Works of Swami Vivekananda, Vol. 4, Advaita Ashrama, 1989.

8

Swami Vivekananda on Education

V. Shirisha

In the present day world the concept of education and the ways of teaching are undergoing tremendous changes, based on science, technology and creativity. It is here to understand the philosophy of education applicable in various in the modern societies. Many thinkers, educationalists had different ways and opinions with regard to education. Sri Aurobindo, Mahatma Gandhi, Jyothiba Phules, Swami Vivekananda, Eshwar Chandra Vidyasagar, Pandit Nehru, Pandit Madan Mohan Malviya and others in the East, Plato, Rousseau, Socrates and others in the west were among such educations and thinkers.

We are also aware of the inadequate facilities in the present educational system. Both Eastern and Western educationalists were engaged for many decades to impart better methods of education and also to boost up the morale of the student community. We are fortunate enough to see one such saint, Swami Vivekananda born in India. Though he lived for a very short period he spoke exclusively on all aspects of life especially on education.

There have been various policies and programmes undertaken in this regard. In this context, we need to understand its philosophy and importance and how it is applicable in the present would order. The present article tried to see the views on education from the view point of Swami Vivekananda.

Importance of Education

To put in the words of Swami Vivekananda "Education is the manifestation of the perfection already in man.[1] Swami Vivekananda has clearly pointed out two aspects in his definition on education.

The above said definition on education is very importance because the word 'manifestation' shows that there is something in man that needs to be expressed. The main aim of learning is to take out the inner ability of a person.

Accordingly, Swami Vivekananda, what a man "learns" is really what he "discovers", by taking the cover off his own soul which is a mine of infinite knowledge.[2]" The other aspect in the definition is the expression, already in man, which talks about individual's talent and capability and potentiality[3]. Knowledge is very much inherent in man. It does not come from outside. It is spiritual in a man's mind but in most of the cases his knowledge is not discovered and used in a proper way. Knowledge is like a fire in a piece of flint, it exists in the mind; suggestion is the friction that brings it out[4]. There are three aspects such as capacity, propensity and capability that emphasise on the matters related to education. There concepts laid according to Israel Scheffler in his book "Of Human Potential", considers the:

1. Capacity is basically to acquire a special feature that someonecan achieve anything that may be possessed by others. For example, you or I might have the capacity

to become a Martina Navratilova, world-famous Tennis player.

2. Propensity shows that an individual is personality can be visible when an opportunity comes and freedom of choice is given. For instance the propensity of Gurudev's Geetanjali shows his inner aspiration to discover the world and its creation.

3. Capability of a person is basically his /hers efficiency and capacity to work for a needed income. It is to see from one's point of view that an individual has so much capacity to get rid of any kind of obstacles.[5]

So far the above discussion is about education and Swami Vivekananda's philosophy, definitions and importance of education, but we go through the aim and goal of education from his perspective.

Aim of Education

The main aim of education is principally laid down by society and differs from one society toanother. He says that education should be spiritual and secular. He says that the present system of education is based on what is said by others rather it is not understood in terms of experience. There is no relation between education and the daily way of living. It is important to acquire education but it is more important to understand the purpose, of education. The main aim, purpose and goal of education are to produce men with character and strength so that they can face any kind of situations and circumstances.

According to him must be able to provide life-building, man-making, character-making assimilation of ideas[6]. To put in his words the real education should enable one to stand on one's own legs[7]. He further goes on and explains that the ideal type of education would be able to produce an integrated and intellectual person who has control over his emotions and stand firm on moral and ethical values.

There are two levels according to ancient Indian philosophy of education, i.e., *para-vidya* and *apara vidya*, which is continuous and complete freedom of soul. The main aim of education is to serve human race, and the duty of acquiring knowledge is a lifelong process. He said that there is a need to study and understand the various branches of knowledge such as our own and also the western. We need to study technical education also, as it gives scope for the establishment of industries that can be useful in providing employment so that one can learn to earn enough for them and save against every rainy day.[8] Swami Vivekananda laid much emphasis on education. The main aim of his education is to make man grow.[9]

His idea of education is to have personal contact with the teacher Gurugriha-vasa. Education which does not help the common man is not worthy. It should make everybody trained so that they can follow and would be of some use to their country. Swami Vivekananda says that, there are some necessary situations and conditions, and there might be so many problems in everybody's life and one should have the strength and courage to tackle such kind of situations and take decisions boldly. A person with strong character may fight against all the odds at his personal and professional fronts whereas a person with no courage would either avoid or try to escape from such kind of situations.

Swami Vivekananda says that the basic value of educations lies in providing foundations of strength, courage, confidence and character in the pupils. The main aim of any educational system is to aspire for higher echelons in life.

Method of Education

Swami Vivekananda, "we want that education by which character is formed, strength of mind is increased, the intellect is expanded, any by which one can stand on one's own feet".

There is only one method to achieve knowledge that is concentration,[10] and the main aim of education is concentration of mind[11] everyone has to follow the same method in attaining knowledge. Knowledge can be acquired only by the power of concentration. To achieve anything in life the total amount of concentration should be high. For example, a cook with better concentration can cook a good meal and the amount of quality and intensity of concentration results in attaining high achievements. In the present condition we are very much distracted and focused on unnecessary thoughts. Major part of our energy is concentrated on unnecessary and distracted thoughts. The key to attain knowledge is only through the power of concentration. He says that the very essence of education is acquiring knowledge through concentration.

Swamiji's Ideas on Education

He says that the present education system is having some merits but with lot of demerits. According to Swami Vivekananda it is of, not a man-making, it is entirely a negative education. A negative education, or any kind of training based on any kind of negativity is worse than death[12]. By observing demerits in the system he came to a conclusion and said that, "we must have life-building, man-making, character-making assimilation of ideas".[13]

After completely understanding the aspects of education, he said imparting knowledge should be the main purpose of education and the main aspects of idea of education is to acquire not only theoretical knowledge but also to achieve high capacities and potentialities in life so as to enhance himself to promote physical intellectual moral and spiritual growth in every individual. He further goes on to explain that every aspect of development and improvising India should first disrupt religion. He says rather indulging the country either in social or in political thoughts it should first absorb spiritual ideas. It is futile to get hold of secular ideas before acquiring spiritual knowledge.

Positive Education

Either in teaching children or while dealing with adults one should have a positive approach Swami Vivekananda said that, only positive ideas and positive knowledge should be imparted to people because negative thoughts weaken people. For instance if a parent consistently nags their child to read, write they might get uninterested and loose interest and curiosity in studies, but if they speak kindly and encourage their children, they will certainly develop themselves. Positive ideas help to improve themselves. One should never point out at the mistakes of others; they only upset and hurt them. Teaching must be changed according to the changing social and economic needs. Shri Ramakrishna encouraged people who were considered worthless, and have changed their lives by inculcating them all the positivity. His words of hope and encouragement, and also his method of teaching was very unique[14].

Swamiji tells education should not inculcate weakness, which is dangerous. People do not know how to make a positive approach. There are good and bad things in every culture and community and only very few people might be better than the other. The most positive approach to life is to have faith and confidence in one's own ability.

A positive approach is very effective in many movements, whether it might be social or religious. According to Swamiji there are three factors that play a vital role in instilling positive approach, such as the family, the school, and the community and the peer group.

In a family, parents come first. The child tries to learn from both the parents, and second is the school, the teacher and their peer-group in the school. The teacher occupies a vital place because after home, i.e., parents the teacher tries to emphasise positive qualities such as love, co-operation, hard work and faith among them.

Many excellent and major achievements in society whether spiritual, physical or social were all community achievements, as it involved thousands of people. Many dams, anicuts, bridges and other scientific inventions and social movements such as female education, ban on drinking etc. are as request of co-operative communities. It is necessary for us to inculcate positive and good habits among children for brighter stronger and courageous nation[15].

Essence of Education

According to Swamiji true education and the core of education is growth and expansion of knowledge but not accumulation of words or as a training of individuals to will rightly and efficiently.[16] Education is not to fill the mind with lot of facts and figures but it is to get mastery over one's own sort i.e.,[-=-- [the ideal of education[17]. To, Swami Vivekananda the very essence of education is concentration of mind, rather collecting fact and figures. He says that if one had to educate themselves they should expand their power of concentration and detachment so that they might be able to collect the facts with strong will and determination. This makes the child to learn and develop the power of concentration.

Education for Character

To put in the words of Swami Vivekananda: "The character of any man is the aggregate of his tendencies, the sum total of the bent of his mind. As pleasure and pain pass before his soul, they leave upon it different pictures and the result of these combined impressions is what is called a man's character. We are what our thought is, if a little hammer blows on our minds, manufacturing out of it what we are wanting it to be. Words are secondary but thoughts arealive and they travel far"[18].

Swamiji says good and bad have equal share in moulding an individual's nature and character. He also clarifies that misery and poverty are great teachers than contentment in life. If we study the autobiographies of great personalities it is clearly understood that suffering have taught them grow. Poverty has given them much more courage and strength to fight rather than prosperity. People who live a luxury life will tend to become soft and weak.

Swamiji compares mind to a lake that, when every wave is risen, at some point of time it do go so low but it does not mean that it will go away forever. There is a possibility that tide may increase. Every man's character is determined by good and bad deeds. His character becomes good and strong only when good impressions exist, where as his character becomes bad when such kind of bad actions prevail on his mind. If a person continuously speaks bad words, thinks bad and does bad his mind will be full of negativity without being conscious he will be influenced by such kind of negativity that in turn affects his character.

He says that education does not meant only acquiring information that is not at all useful in life. He says that, such kind of education should be imparted to people that should be life-building, man making and character and assimilation of ideas. Swamiji says that education should strengthen character and mind. Education should enable people to equip themselves to meet the needs of daily life.

Education that does not teach charity, character building is not worth at all. According to Swamji the best and ideal education is character building but we are only trying to polish outside rather developing our inner self. He said that the present system of education is not that good. In ancient India students never use to pay to teachers. They stayed at their homes and learnt, that is taught, but now the students have to pay fees and learn. There is no proper and personal interaction between the pupil and the teacher. There was no difference between thought and action and theory and practice. Those times schools focussed on community, intellect and talent and culture. High ideas were left before the students and emphasis was much on practicing such ideas and daily life. The teachers also used self-experience as a method of learning.

Swamijis idea of education is personal contact with the teacher-Gurgriha-Vasa. Without the personal life of a teacher there would be no education. He also goes on explaining the fact that the universities have not produced even a single creative man, they provided only an examining body. The idea of sacrificing for the common good is yet to be developed in our country[19].

Swami Vivekananda wanted both moral and intellectual education. He said that education should make people more self-reliant so that one can be able to stand on their feet.

There are defects in the present system of education. It is just making checks out of an individual. They wanted to mastery over every aspect but they do not know their fore fathers be up to. A nation that has no history of its own has nothing in the world and cannot achieve anything. One has to make their nation pride. According to him people should learn technological skills so that they can earn their livelihood, instead of wasting time by requesting others[20].

After going through various countries in the world Swami Vivekananda observed that education is the only thing that change one's own faith, it has the power to eradicate poverty of the masses. No country can progress without the spread of education. He said that the present society, has though has some merits, but it is full of negative points. It is entirely a negative education, not a man-making education. Any kind of negativity is worth than death. Nothing can be achieved without the spread of education.

Female Education

Anything for the improvement of a society can be achieved only through female education. Women students must be trained in ethical and spiritual life. With the help of science, women should be taught history, Puranas, house-keeping, acts and duties and principles of home-life for a better ideal character development. Great men are born only in the homes of education and pious mothers[21]. Education of females will be ideal and it can act as a catalyst to solve most of the problems. Women can solve their own problems with the education they acquired. In the present system it is necessary to learn self-defence. See how and the queen of Jhansi, Rani Laxmi Bai,[22] Kaikeyi and Satyabhama who supported Dasaratha and Sri Krishna in the battle field. In India, home is identified with mother. Womanhood in India played a very crucial role because Indian mothers are ready to sacrifice anything for the betterment and benefit of children. In ancient India women were free, educated and respected and held a very high place, even, in Upanishads there is a mention about it. Women like Maitreyi, Gargi and others who attained scholarly knowledge challenged men also. Whereas restrictions on them began only after the Muslim invasions and their social status gradually got degraded and became to that of slaves by men[23].

After going through Vedas, Upanishads and other texts and also observing the position throughout the world wherever he visited, swami Vivekananda came to a conclusion that the reason for downfall in India is mainly due to neglect of masses and women. Swami Vivekananda's national regeneration programme stressed on emancipation of women and upliftment of masses[24].

Many countries in the world have become great because of their respect for women. A country that does not respect will never have any future. No country can be prosperous unless women's condition is improved and their welfare is noticed.

Indian women face so many problems, but they can be solved by attaining education[25]. Educate your women first and leave them to themselves, then they will tell you was what reforms are necessary for them[26]. Women should be given education and left to themselves so that they can resolve their own issues and problems and learn to fight back with all energy. Education alone can make them self-dependent. They should be taught the things that benefit them and also others.

Swami Vivekananda was worried about the degrading status of women. He said that any sense of alienation of women will destroy the development of a country. He gave high importance to women education by inculcating spiritual values in them. He said some consider ideal women Sita, Savitri, Ma Durga and the mother Sharada Devi. In India women's position is miserable when we see America where women are learned and free. He urged that there is a clear discrimination between men and women in all aspects. Swamiji has clearly foreseen the future of our country before a hundred years, then stressed on educating women and the masses who are the foundation pillars of our country (or any nation).

Conclusion

There have been numerous changes in the society; especially remarkable changes took place in the system of education since Swami Vivekananda foresaw the future of a nation in creating an individual with knowledge, concentration, action and work. We can say that such a major change occurred in our country to fulfill one of his dreams. 'The Right to education for everyone', was guaranteed by the Constitution of India, through it still has to reach the people, but such initiative was taken by the government. His idea of education for the underprivileged, economically weak also for women saw a positive response. Various governments of various nations have taken measures to improve the plight of such people. Swami Vivekananda was very much concerned about the weak and poor. He also suggested that some drastic policychanges should be taken by the nations to develop such people, as their development is society's and nation's, development. He also said that education is starting now in the world but civilisation has yet to be started. He stressed that unless basic needs and primary needs are fulfilled and no nation can be prosperous, and this all can happen only through education. Though Government of India has taken measures to redress the grievances of the weak, underprivileged, it started providing them with reservations that is yet to reach top position that such communities would be benefited. Women reservations at some levels are implemented; on the whole women reservation bill is yet to get a nod. Many schools and colleges started imparting the process of learning different from that of earlier one though some changes have taken place. Swami Vivekananda's dream for the 'ideas of life-long education, character-building education, education that is for the upliftment and betterment of women should yet to be fulfilled. Swamiji was a great visionary and educational thinker who imagined these noble ideas before a hundred years when no nation could have such progressive ideas and thoughts.

References

1. "*The Complete Works of Swami Vivekananda, Mayawati*", Memorial Edition, 1962, Advaita Ashram, Madras, Volume No. 4, p. 358.
2. *Ibid.,* p. 28.
3. Dr. Kiran Walia, Swami Vivekananda, "My Idea of EDUCATION", Advaita Ashrama, Kolkata, 2008, p. 7.
4. T.S. Avinashilingam, EDUCATION COMPILED FROM THE SPEECHES AND WRITINGS OF SWAMI VIVEKANANDA, Sri Ramakrishna Math, Madras, 2011, p. 8.
5. Dr. Kiran Walia, op.cit., p.18.
6. *Ibid.,* p. 19.
7. "THE COMPLETE WORKS OF SWAMI VIVEKANANDA, MAYAWATI, MEMORIAL EDITION", 1962, Advaita Ashram, Madras, C.W. Vol. 14, pp. 367-8.
8. *Ibid.,* Vol. 2, p. 15.
9. *Ibid.,* Vol. 2, p. 130.
10. *Ibid.,* Vol. 6, p. 38.
11. C.W., Vol. 3, 8th Ed. p. 301.
12. *Ibid.,* p. 302.
13. C.W. VII, pp. 170-171.
14. *Ibid.,* p. 23.
15. Swami Vivekananda, MY INDIA, THE INDIA ETERNAL, Ramakrishna Mission Institute of Culture, Kolkata, 2010, p. 55.
16. *Ibid.,* p. 56.
17. T.S. Avinashilingam, Educational Philosophy of Swami Vivekananda, Sri Ramakrishna Mission Vidyalaya, Coimbatore, 1997, p. 69.
18. *Ibid.,* n. 15, p. 57.
19. T.S. Avinashilingam, op.cit., pp. 43-46.
20. Swami Vivekananda, op.cit., pp. 61-62.
21. C.W. VI, p. 489.
22. C.W. III pp. 302-303.
23. T.S. Avinashilingam, op.cit., pp. 178-179.
24. The Masters as I Saw Him, p. 286.
25. Swami Vivekananda, op.cit, p. 71.
26. C.W., Vol. VI, p. 115.

9

The Relevance of Swami Vivekananda's Thoughts on Education in 21st Century India

Niharika Tiwari

Swami Vivekananda said:

"We want that education by which character is formed, strength of mind is increased, the intellect is expanded, and by which one can stand on one's own feet".

Swami Vivekananda (1863-1902) was born into an aristocratic Bengali family of Calcutta. He showed an inclination towards spirituality and God realisation. Shri Ramakrishna, his spiritual teacher taught him *"Advaita Vedanta"* (non-dualism); that all religions are true and that service to man was the most effective worship of God. Brought up and educated in 19th century Calcutta, Vivekananda was introduced at an early age to the principles of western thinking, which taught one should not accept anything without evidence. Although he was a brilliant student and was well-versed in history, philosophy, literature and contemporary western thought, he held firmly to the idea: "Do not believe a thing because another has said it is so. Find out the truth for yourself. That is realisation[1]." In order to realise the truth he studied different religious and philosophical thoughts of the east and the west both. He visited several religious leaders as well as to find out the truth. Ultimately, he met Shri Ramakrishna at the Dakshineswar temple garden near Calcutta. This meeting with Ramkrishna proved to be a turning point in Narendra's life. He trained Vivekananda in a number of disciplines along with providing him great spiritual power.

After the death of his guru, Vivekananda became a wandering monk, extensively touring the Indian subcontinent and acquiring first-hand knowledge of the conditions that prevailed in India. With the passage of time, his intellectual skepticism and argumentative nature were gradually transformed into self-surrender, faith and devotion. He later visited to the United States and represented India as a delegate in the 1893 Parliament of World Religions at Chicago and spread the message of spirituality there too. He delivered several public and private lectures disseminating true tenets of Hindu philosophy, worldwide. He also established the Vedanta societies in America and England. The main emphasis of his vision was to reveal the essence of a good life before the world in terms of Indian spiritualism for which he emphasised the Philosophy of *Vedanta*.

The main focus of this paper is to explore the relevance of Swami Vivekananda's thoughts on education in terms of modern education system and society in India. It will explore how Vivekananda's vision of education can fill the existing lacunas of our 21st century's education system, for making it more capable in addressing the problems of this country.

Without any reservation, it can be accepted that our education system has touched new heights as far as modern, professional and scientific education are concerned. Our professional minds are spread all over the world. At domestic level we are trying to eradicate gender and caste based disparities in the field of education by universalising the basic education with the help of various affirmative actions such as right to education, reservation system etc. What I mentioned here are basically the methods to fulfill the 'instrumental role' of education in our life, i.e., the use of education to achieve certain predetermined goals say higher literacy level or employment etc. Unfortunately, 'substantial role' of education that is to inculcate the values of humanity, integrity of character, and compassion is getting eroded from our education system. We have very intelligent doctors, but nobody knows when he/she would sell the kidney of a patient. Similarly, our corrupt politicians, administrators, sexually perverted youngsters, well educated terrorists, all have been the part of our education system at one point of time or the other. These vacuums can be filled by accompanying our modern education system with the Swami Vivekananda's vision of education, which is deeply grounded in his philosophy of Vedanta and Karma Yoga.

Philosophy of Vedanta: This philosophy says that the true essence of human beings lies in their soul. Therefore, a close and positive co-ordination between human body, mind and soul is imperative to realise the true meaning of a good life. The mass of knowledge called Vedanta was discovered by *rishis*-the spiritual discoverers. "The mass writings of the Vedas consists of two parts-the '*Karma Kanda'* and the '*Jnana Kanda*', i.e., the work portion and the knowledge portion. The work portion consists of various sacrifices. Most of them of late have been given up as not practicable under present circumstances, but others remain to the present day in some shape or other. The main ideas of Karma Kanda, which consists of the duties of man, the duties of the student . . . present day. But the spiritual portion of our Vedas is in the second part, the Jnana Kanda, the Vedanta, the end of

Vedas. The essence of the knowledge of the Vedas was called by the name Vedanta" (Chetanananda, 2009).

Vedanta claims that man is divine, that all this which we see around us is the outcome of that consciousness of the divine. Everything that is strong and powerful in human nature is the outcome of that divinity, and though potential in many, there is no difference between man and man essentially, all being alike divine.

Vedanta also preaches ethics and morality, a very important part of our life, which is getting deteriorated from our education system gradually. He said, purify yourself, and the world is bound to purify itself. This is the idea needed to be taught now more than ever before. The world will change if we change. The question is why I should see evil in others. I cannot see evil unless I am evil. I cannot be miserable unless I am weak. This is called attaining freedom in Vedanta. One should remain same in misery and happiness, success and defeat.

Philosophy of Karma Yoga: The word Karma is derived from the Sanskrit "*Kri*", means 'to do'; all action is *Karma*. Technically, this word also means the effects of actions. In connection with metaphysics, it sometimes means the effects of which our past actions were the causes. But in Karma-Yoga we have simply to do with the word Karma as meaning work. The goal of mankind is knowledge. That is the one ideal placed before us by Eastern philosophy. Pleasure is not the goal of man, but knowledge. Pleasure and happiness come to an end. It is a mistake to suppose that pleasure is the goal.

'The cause of all the miseries, we have in the world is that men foolishly think pleasure to be the ideal to strive for that. After a long time man finds that it is not real happiness, but knowledge, towards which he is going, and that both pleasure and pain are great teachers, and that he learns as much from evil as from good. As pleasure and pain pass before his soul they have upon it different pictures, and the result of these combined impressions is what is called man's "character". If one takes the character of any man, it really is but the aggregate of tendencies, the sum total of the bent of his mind; one will find that misery and happiness are equal factors in the formation of that character. Good and evil have an equal share in moulding character, and in some instances misery is a greater teacher than happiness. In studying the great characters the world has produced. I dare to say, in the vast majority of cases, it would be found that it was misery that taught more than happiness. It was poverty that taught more than wealth, it was blows that brought out their inner fire more than praise. Now this knowledge, again, is inherent in man. No knowledge comes from outside; it is all inside. What we say a man "knows", should in strict psychological language, be what he "discovers" or "unveils". What a man "learns" is really what he "discovers", by taking the cover off his own soul, which is a mine of infinite knowledge[2].

Objective of Education: The goal of education envisaged by Swami Vivekananda can be found in the Memorandum of Association of Ramkrishna Mission established by Swami Vivekananda. There are following objectives of the Ramakrishna Mission which was founded in May 1897. The Memorandum of Association says (Sanyal, 2012):

(a) To impart and promote the study of the Vedanta and its principles as propounded by Sri Ramakrishna and practically illustrated by his own life, and of comparative theology in its widest form.

(b) To impart and promote the study of the arts, sciences, and industries.

(c) To train teachers in all branches of knowledge above-mentioned and enable them to reach the masses.

(d) To carry on educational work among the masses.

(e) To establish, maintain, carry on, and assist schools, colleges, orphanages, workshops, laboratories, hospitals, dispensaries, houses for the infirm, the invalid and afflicted, famine relief works, and other educational and charitable works, and institutions of a like nature.

(f) To print and publish and to sell or distribute gratuitously or otherwise, journals, periodicals, books or leaflets, that the Association may think desirable for the promotion of its objects.

(g) To incorporate any institutions, societies, or associations having objects wholly or in part similar to any of those of the Association, and to co-operate with any person or persons in aid of such objects.

Vivekananda's Vision on Education: His vision on education has its genesis in Vedanta and Karma Yoga. Moreover, the Memorandum of the Mission also reflects that the real objective of the education can be reached only by following the path of Vedanta and Karma Yoga. He said, the nature of education should be such as to provide the nourishment to the character, mind, intellect and livelihood to an individual and society. The prime aim of education is to achieve fullness of perfection already present in a child. He also professed that education should be able to maintain "Unity in Diversity", a notion that is very important for 21st century's terrorism ridden world. He emphasised that education can never be separated from spirituality.

His meaning of spirituality neither stands for dogmatic religious teachings nor does he oppose material aspect of education. For him spirituality stands for humanity and it is rooted in his philosophy of Vedanta. Therefore, Swami Vivekananda visualised that all sort of national as well as global challenges can be addressed if spirituality remains one of the fundamental constituents of our education system. Moreover, he suggested that education should be mental and physical both. It should make a person capable of winning his/her inner weakness such as lust and ego. He emphasised that only putting information in the minds of students is not the objective of education, because it will lead to the lopsided development of one's personality. He insisted on a comprehensive education consisting of education of masses as well. He never separated religion from education as he considered religion a medium to find out the truth.

Swamiji[3] has also said that a teacher plays a role model for his/her disciples. Therefore, a teacher should always aspire to put a clear cut objective of education before his/her students and to help them to grow to perfection.

Women and Education: *"By no means, said the Swamiji, 'but our right of interference is limited entirely to giving education. Women must be put in a position to solve their own problems in their own way. No one can or ought to do this for them. And our Indian women are as capable of doing it as any in the world"*[4]. He was a great supporter of women empowerment. He not only advocated for education but for functional education for women in order to make them capable to comprehend and to confront the challenges posed in every walk of life. *"Observing the state of women's education in India, Swamiji lamented that he could not understand why so much difference was made between men and women, especially when Vedanta declared that one and the same Self was present in all beings. He quoted Manu to assert that daughters should be supported and educated with as much care and attention as the sons. This discrimination* *is made in every part of our society even now. It is not only in India. This malady is present all over the world. French and Swiss women got their voting rights not long ago. However, the fact is that all nations have attained greatness by paying proper respect to women. Swamiji therefore demanded forcefully that women must be put in a position so that they could solve their problems in their own way. Why not? Our Indian women are as capable of doing it as any other women in the world. These were Swamiji's bold words uttered in the 19th century. Look at the life of Sri Sarada Devi, the Holy Mother—how powerful she had been spiritually! Swamiji therefore urged his followers to spread female education the absence of which caused to a great extent India's degeneration. He pointed out unerringly that it was only in the homes of educated and pious mothers that great men and women were born*" (Sanyal, 2012).

In *My Idea of Education*, Swami Vivekananda emphasises on the control of one's mind, desire, and will to reach a disciplined state of higher, esoteric knowledge. In the book, he states that this can be achieved by strengthening one's power of concentration through meditation and purity of the mind and soul. Vivekananda also espouses the theory of '*Brahmacharya*', which also comes into play here, as he says that the concept of detachment from all things worldly is a necessary prerequisite to be the master commander of true knowledge. On the basis of above descriptions following crucial role of education can be identified in the background of Swami Vivekananda's thoughts:

Character Building: Swamiji emphasised that a strong character building is important for a confident and strong personality. It enhances the will power of a person. He said good character is the basis of a promising personality. In the absence of good character one cannot realise his/her true self.

Spiritual and Moral Development of Personality: Since Vedanta and Karma Yoga are the epistemological source of the Swamiji's vision of education. It is imperative that spiritual and moral elements will definitely be given much importance. His vision of education denied orthodox and narrow vision of the concepts of spirituality and morality. He advocated the secular role of spirituality and morality leading to the development of a balanced (intellectual, moral and intellectual) personality.

To Nurture Values of Humanity: He emphasised that values of humanity should be taught as integral part of our education system. Thus, the horizon of education system can be broadened, by incorporating both substantial and instrumental role of education in human life. It can be helpful in bringing out one's true human values for the well being of the society.

Physical and Intellectual Development: Swami Vivekananda was a strong votary of metal as well as physical development of personality. He believed that a perfect education must profess the development of both mind as well as the body in order to provide healthy citizens to the nation. According to him, only a healthy person can feel, think, analyse and work in a co-ordinated way.

To Develop Confluence of Science and Religion: He never opposed scientific education and tried to develop a symbiosis between the two. He said, scientific education is important for material development of the society. Whereas religious teachings make the value system of the society stronger. He called religion **'The Universal Science[5]'**. He said, "*All narrow, limited, fighting ideas of religion must be given up.... The religious ideals of the future must embrace all that exists in the world and is good and great, and at the same time, have infinite scope for future development. All* *that was good in the past must be preserved; and the doors must be kept open for future additions to the already existing store. Religion (and science are included under this name) must also be inclusive, and not look down with contempt upon one another, because their particular ideals of God are different* (Rolland, 2009)."

To Provide Traditional as well as Vocational Knowledge and Skills: He emphasised the importance of one's traditional cultural knowledge, as it makes one feel proud of one's great traditions. But he never undermined the role of modern vocational education. He said vocational education is helpful in eradicating poverty, unemployment etc. It makes people self dependent and honest in terms of material aspects.

Methods to Achieve the Goal of Education: The ways suggested by Swamiji to achieve the perfect education are multi-dimensional. It is the method (course-structure and pedagogy) which is basically being aimed to be achieved in our country to strengthen the education system. It involves a symbiosis of intellect, body and soul. Moreover, the methods of teaching should be rooted in the great ancient Indian tradition. The revival of 'Nalanda University' can be a positive step in this direction. He professed that Pupils should be made capable to develop their own perceptions, rather than mugging up through books. Meditation, concentration of mind through practice of yoga, lectures, discussions, experiences of daily life and creative activities should be the methods of teaching. Pupils should be trained to solve the problems of their day to day life. The above mention methods are useful in today's system of education because it develops democratic values and creativity in the students. Moreover, course structure and pedagogy both should be inter-disciplinary.

Relevance in the 21st Century: If we really want to build a peaceful society which is free from hatred, corruption, ego, violence etc. it is mandatory for us to incorporate Swamiji's vision of education in the present education system. The ways suggested by Swamiji can be included in today's education system by organizing workshops on value education. Teachers should take it as their fundamental duty to make their students understand the importance of human values and spirituality while teaching any discipline. Definitely, it will help us in the process of nation building which is still in the transitional phase. There are following grounds illustrating the relevance of Swamiji's vision of education in 21st century India:

Violence Free Society: If values of humanity, morality and spirituality are integrated in the modern education system, which is presently shrouded by instrumental objectives, the dream of a society free from physical, psychological and structural violence[6] can be materialised to a large extent.

Integrity of Character and Personality: Notion of Vedanta and Karma Yoga, if taught to the pupils at a very beginning level of their schooling, it can provide them a good character and formulate integrated personality. Karma Yoga practicing people will never enter into realm of crime and brutality.

Development of a Balanced Society: If the objective of education as envisaged by Swami Vivekananda is incorporated in the education system of India. Our society will be able to get democratised rapidly. Because, he has advocated the accessibility of education to all irrespective of caste, class and gender based stratifications.

To Generate Strong Will Power: Absence of the capacity to instill strong will-power in the mind and character of the people of this country has been one of the biggest flaws of our education system. Today, people who are wielding power to lead the country do not have strong will power, which results into socio-economic and political degeneration of our nation. Basically, it can be generated only in the presence of spirituality and morality. Therefore, the relevance of Swamiji's thoughts on education cannot be denied.

Bed-rock of a Multi-cultural Society: An inter-disciplinary education develops a balanced mind-set in the society, by providing information about the ethos of a multi-cultural society. Pupils nurtured under such environment have a secular approach to maintain the fabrics of a multicultural society. Where every citizen will think beyond the boundaries of self and education will not be considered merely a source of collecting and transferring information. Instead of that, it will spread the values of humanity as the sole objective of education.

The structures and functions of 21st century's education system in our country are famous world-wide for providing the best vocational and instrumental educations. At the same time, our moral values and ethics are getting depreciated due to increased consumerism and materialistic culture in globalised India. Now a day's people have started giving priority to material interests over human values. As increasing number of cases about the incidents of murder, rape, pedophilic incidents and corruption in public life have illustrated. On the basis of Swamiji's vision it can be said that, education is the only way to bring out the true human values present in one's soul. Due to his profound vision about the world, he *is rightly called the philosopher-saint of India. His brilliant ideas on education give us an insight into the mind of the true revolutionary, Swami Vivekananda.*

References

1. The Life of Swami Vivekananda by His Eastern and Western Disciples, Vol. 1, 31.
2. http://www.ramakrishnavivekananda.info/vivekananda/volume_1/vol_1_frame.htm
3. Swami Vivekananda is also called "Swamiji".
4. On Indian Women—their Past, Present and Future (Prabuddha Bharata, December, 1898).
5. The Life of Vivekananda and the Universal Gospel, 2009, p. 214.
6. It consists of caste, gender, ethnicity and religion based inequalities leading to the deprivation of the people.

Further Reading

Chetananand, Swami (2009), *"Vedanta Voice of Freedom"*, Advaita Ashram Publication Department, Kolkata.

Complete Works of Swami Vivekananda Vol. III. URL:http://vsc.iitm.ac.in/Vivekananda/Complete%20works/Complete_Works_of_ Swami_ Vivekananda_-_Vol_3.pdf.

Complete Works of Swami Vivekananda Vol. I.

http://www.ramakrishnavivekananda.info/vivekananda/volume_1/vol_1_frame.htm.

On Indian Women—Their Past, Present and Future (*Prabuddha Bharata, December, 1898*).

Rolland, Romain (2009), "*The Life of Vivekananda and The Universal Gospal*", Advaita Ashram Publication Department, Kolkata.

Sanyal B. K. (2012), "Revisiting Educational Thoughts and Actions of Swami Vivekananda"

URL: www.sriramakrishna.org/.../_bulletin_...

Vivekanand, Swami (2010) "*My Idea of Education*" Paperback, Advaita Ashrama Publication, Kolkata.

10

Swami Vivekananda and Hinduism

Seema Mathur

Swami Vivekananda is one of the most admired spiritual leaders of India. The world knows him as an inspiring Hindu monk and Hindus consider him as a source of spiritual power, mental energy, strength-giving and open-mindedness.[1]

Vivekananda was born on January 12, 1863, in a middle-class Bengali family of Calcutta. His father, Vishwanath Datta, was a successful attorney with interests in a wide range of subjects, and his mother, Bhuvaneshwari Devi, was endowed with deep devotion, strong character and other qualities.[2] Narendranath Dutt, as he was called before sainthood, had acquired a vast knowledge of different subjects, especially Western philosophy and history and also associated with "Brahmo Movement" for some time. Vivekananda found his guru in Sri Ramakrishna Paramhansa,when he askeda question to Sri Ramakrishna *"Sir, have you seen God?"* Without a moment's hesitation, Sri Ramakrishna replied: "*Yes, I have. I see him as clearly as I see you, only in a much intense sense.*" Sri Ramakrishna instilled in their pupils the spirit of renunciation and brotherly love for one another. After passing of his 'Guru' Sri Ramakrishna Narendra formed a new monastic brotherhood, and in 1887 he took the formal vows of *sannyasa*and became famous as Swami Vivekananda. On theurge of own inherent powers Swamiji toured across India to know his country and people.

He was the first religious leader in India to understand and openly declare that the real cause of India's downfall was the neglect of the masses. The immediate need was to provide food and other bare necessities of life to the hungry millions. For this they should be taught improved methods of agriculture, village industries, etc. It was in this context that Vivekananda grasped the crux of the problem of poverty in India owing to centuries of oppression; the downtrodden masses had lost faith in their capacity to improve their lot. It was first of all necessary to infuse into their minds faith in them. For this they needed a life-giving, inspiring message. Swamiji found this message in the principle of the Atman, the doctrine of the potential divinity of the soul, taught in *Vedanta*, the ancient system of religious philosophy of India. He saw that, in spite of poverty, the masses clung to religion, but they had never been taught the life-giving, ennobling principles of Vedanta and how to apply them in practical life.Thus the masses needed two kinds of knowledge: secular knowledge to improve their economic condition and spiritual knowledge to infuse in them faith in themselves and strengthen their moral sense. The next question was how to spread these two kinds of knowledge among the masses? Through education – this was the answer that Swamiji found.One thing became clear to Swamiji: to carry out his plans for the spread of education and for the uplift of the poor masses, and also of women, an efficient organisation of dedicated people was needed. As he said later on, he wanted "to set in motion machinery which will bring noblest ideas to the doorstep of even the poorest and the meanest." It was to serve as this 'machinery' that Swamiji founded the Ramakrishna Mission a few years later.

Swami Vivekananda got a right forum in the World's Parliament of Religions in Chicago in 1893 to present his Master's message to the world. His speeches made him world famous as an 'orator by divine right' and as a 'messenger of Indian wisdom to the Western world'. (See the full speech in World's Parliament of Religions.[3])

After returning to India in January 1897 Swamiji lectured widely on the east coast and in the mid- West, and also took trips to England and Franceto rouse the religious consciousness of the people. And create in them pride in their cultural heritage to bring about unification of Hinduism by pointing out the common bases of its sects; and to focus the attention of educated people on the plight of the down trodden masses, and to expound his plan for their uplift by the application of the principles of Practical Vedanta.He founded Ramakrishna Mission, in which monks and lay people would jointly undertake propagation of Practical Vedanta, and various forms of social service, such as running hospitals, schools, colleges, hostels, rural development centres etc., and conducting massive relief and rehabilitation work for victims of earthquakes, cyclones and other calamities, in different parts of India and other countries. In Belur Swami Vivekananda established Ramakrishna Math, which is open to all men without any distinction of religion, race or caste. Swamiji spent his life for inspiring and guiding people, both monastic and lay. Before his Mahasamadhi on the 4th of July, 1902 at the young age of 39 he had written to followers: "*It may be that I shall find it good to get outside my body, to cast it off like a worn out garment. But I shall not cease to work. I shall inspire men everywhere until the whole world shall know that it is one with God.*"[4]

Ideas about Hinduism

It was Swami Vivekananda who gave to Hinduism as a whole a clear-cut identity, a distinct profile. Before Swamiji came Hinduism was a loose confederation of many different sects. Swamiji was the first religious leader to speak about the common bases of Hinduism and the common ground of all sects. He was the first person, as guided by his Master Sri Ramakrishna, to accept all Hindu doctrines and the views of all Hindu philosophers and sects as different aspects of one total view of Reality and way of life known as Hinduism. Speaking about Swamiji's role in giving Hinduism its distinct identity, Sister Nivedita wrote: *"... it may be said that when he began to speak it was of 'the religious ideas of the Hindus', but when he ended, Hinduism had been created."* There was a lot of quarrel and competition among the various sects of Hinduism and the protagonists of different systems and schools of philosophy were claiming their views to be the only true and valid ones. But by applying Sri Ramakrishna's doctrine of Harmony (Samanvaya) Swamiji brought about an overall unification of Hinduism on the basis of the principle of unity in diversity. About Swamiji's role to unite Hinduism K. M. Pannikar, the eminent historian and diplomat, wrote: *"This new Shankaracharya may well be claimed to be a unifier of Hindu ideology."*

Making an objective assessment of Swami Vivekananda's contributions to world culture,[5] the eminent British historian A. L. Basham stated that *"in centuries to come, he will be remembered as one of the main molders of the modern world..."* One of the most significant contributions of Swami Vivekananda to the modern world is his interpretation of religion as a universal experience of transcendent Reality, common to all humanity. Swamiji met the challenge of modern science by showing that religion is as scientific as science itself; religion is the 'science of consciousnesses. As such, religion and science are not contradictory to each other but are complementary.

This universal conception frees religion from the hold of superstitions, dogmatism, priest craft and intolerance, and makes religion the highest and noblest pursuit - the pursuit of supreme Freedom, supreme Knowledge, and supreme Happiness. Vivekananda's concept of 'potential divinity of the soul' gives a new, ennobling concept of man. The present age is the age of humanism, which holds that man should be the chief concern and center of all activities and thinking. Through science and technology man has attained great prosperity and power, and modern methods of communication and travel have converted human society into a 'global village'. But the degradation of man has also been going on apace, as witnessed by the enormous increase in broken homes, immorality, violence, crime, etc., in modern society.

Vivekananda's concept of potential divinity of the soul prevents this degradation, divinises human relationships, and makes life meaningful and worth living. Swamiji has laid the foundation for 'spiritual humanism', which is manifesting itself through several neo-humanistic movements and the current interest in meditation, Zen etc., all over the world.The prevalent morality, in both individual life and social life, is mostly based on fear - fear of the police, fear of public ridicule, fear of God's punishment, fear of Karma, and so on. The current theories of ethics also do not explain why a person should be moral and be good to others.

Vivekananda has given a new theory of ethics and new principle of morality based on the intrinsic purity and oneness of the Atman. We should be pure because purity is our real nature, our true divine Self or Atman. Similarly, we should love and serve our neighbours because we are all one in the Supreme spirit known as Paramatman or Brahman. Another great contribution of Swami Vivekananda was to build a bridge between Indian culture and Western culture. He did it by interpreting Hindu scriptures and philosophy and the Hindu way of life and institutions to the Western people in an idiom, which they could understand. He made the Western people realise that they had to learn much from Indian spirituality for their own well-being. He showed that, in spite of her poverty and backwardness, India had a great contribution to make to world culture. In this way he was instrumental in ending India's cultural isolation from the rest of the world. He was India's first great cultural ambassador to the West.

On the other hand, Swami's interpretation of ancient Hindu scriptures, philosophy, institutions, etc prepared the mind of Indians to accept and apply in practical life two best elements of Western culture, namely science and technology and humanism. Swamiji has taught Indians how to master Western science and technology and at the same time develop spiritually. Swamiji has also taught Indians how to adapt Western humanism (especially the ideas of individual freedom, social equality and justice and respect for women) to Indian ethos.

In spite of her innumerable linguistic, ethnic, historical and regional diversities, India has had from time immemorial a strong sense of cultural unity. It was, however, Swami Vivekananda who revealed the true foundations of this culture and thus clearly defined and strengthened the sense of unity as a nation. Swamiji gave Indians proper understanding of their country's great spiritual heritage and thus gave them pride in their past. Furthermore, he pointed out to Indians the drawbacks of Western culture and the need for India's contribution to overcome these drawbacks.

In this way Swamiji made India a nation with a global mission. Sense of unity, pride in the past, sense of mission – these were the factors, which gave real strength and purpose to India's nationalist movement. Several eminent leaders of India's freedom movement have acknowledged their indebtedness to Swamiji. Free India's first Prime Minister

Jawaharlal Nehru wrote: *"Rooted in the past, full of pride in India's prestige, Vivekananda was yet modern in his approach to life's problems, and was a kind of bridge between the past of India and her present ... he came as a tonic to the depressed and demoralised Hindu mind and gave it self-reliance and some roots in the past."*Netaji Subhash Chandra Bose wrote: "*Swamiji harmonised the East and the West, religion and science, past and present. And that is why he is great. Our countrymen have gained unprecedented self-respect, self-reliance and self-assertion from his teachings.*"

Swamiji's most unique contribution to the creation of new India was to open the minds of Indians to their duty to the downtrodden masses. Long before the ideas of Karl Marx were known in India, Swamiji spoke about the role of the laboring classes in the production of the country's wealth. He was the first religious leader in India to speak for the masses, formulate a definite philosophy of service, and organise large-scale social service. Vivekananda did not merely interpret ancient Hindu scriptures and philosophical ideas in terms of modern thought. He also added several illuminating original concepts based on his own transcendental experiences and vision of the future.

Similarly, Vivekananda learnt from his Master that all religions in the world were phases of one eternal religion. The conflating of India, its soil and Hindu religiosity is accomplished with a flourish, something that would become part and parcel of Vivekananda's politically charged conception of Hinduism.

There is a clear identification between Vivekananda and the view that religions might differ in word, ritual, doctrine and emphasis but all faiths are ultimately paths to the same god. In many of his public pronouncements, he explicitly seeks to convey that his message was one of peace and a united religion and not of antagonism. Having studied comparative religions, he finds all faiths to have had the same foundations as his own faith. If there were differences, these were in the realm of the non-essential elements within faiths. Going a step further, he wants a plurality of faiths in the world to suit a variety of contexts. Here, Vivekananda is talking about the desirability of different faiths:

"I do not deprecate the existence of sects in the world. Would to god there were twenty million more, for the more there are, there will be a greater field for selection. What I do object to is trying to fit one religion to every case. Though all religions are essentially the same, they must have the varieties of form produced by dissimilar circumstances among different nations."[6]

This sounds perfectly reasonable. It is worth marking that he calls them "sects" and not religions. But the overall tone and tenor is one of remarkable liberality. Now read the last line of the quote: *"We must each have our own individual religion, individual so far as the externals of it go."* The plurality of faiths, then, is limited to the externals. Remove the externals and what will emerge is a universal faith defined by Vivekananda, based entirely on his reading of the Vedanta. The Vedantic ideal of Oneness and the Universal Soul would ultimately prevail. In the words of Swamiji, "*When we shall feel that oneness, we shall be immortal. We are physically immortal even, one with the universe. So long as there is one that breathes throughout the universe, I live in that one. I am not this limited little being, I am the universal. I am the life of all the sons of the past. I am the soul of Buddha, of Jesus, of Mohammed.*" When the argument for a single universal faith had to be made strenuously, Vivekananda abandons even the "*We must each have our own individual religion*" rhetoric with alacrity: *"There never was my religion or yours, my national religion or your national religion; there never existed many religions, there is only the one. One infinite religion existed all through eternity and will ever exist, and this religion is expressing itself in various countries, in various ways."* What, then, about the argument that promised to accommodate even twenty million or more sects in the world, even if this acceptance of plurality was only based on the acknowledgement of a multitude of external forms of religion? The above quote ends with the following sentence: "Therefore we must respect all religions and we must try to accept them all as far as we can." The respect for other religions was, therefore, conditional. It depended on phrases like "so far as the externals of it go" and "as far as we can".

Vivekananda argues that Nature always represents unity in variety, that *"...through all these variations of the phenomenal runs the Infinite, the Unchangeable, the Absolute Unity"*. What was true of Nature is also true for humans: *"...the microcosm is but a miniature repetition of the macrocosm."* This is the reason, affirms Vivekananda, why no man's faith ought to be disturbed. While this too sounds utterly reasonable, it also is part of the same trajectory where other faiths are limited and inadequate and require getting *"hold of a man where he stands and giving him a push upwards"*. Oneness, Absolute Unity and the necessary push upwards were possible, though, only if a set of preconditions were met and unambiguously affirmed.

Vivekananda wants to find a way of bringing about a fusion between races and tribes, especially so because he finds them to be unequal in culture. Similarly, a profusion of languages ought to have a common link. In Sanskrit, *"a great sacred language of which all others would be considered as manifestations"*, he located and found the most viable linguistic solution. The common rubric under which he attempts to club all the races and tribes was found in the term '*Aryan*'. Even the distinction between *Aryan* and *Dravidian* was casually brushed aside as merely a philological one and not of race and blood. Once language and race were unified, the asymmetry between cultures had to be rectified: *"Just as Sanskrit has been the linguistic solution, so the Aryan the racial solution. So the Brahmanism is the solution of the varying degrees of progress and culture as well as that of all social and political problems."*

In his paper on 'Hinduism' Swami Vivekananda says that the three religions stand in the world, which have come down from time prehistoric—Hinduism, Zoroastrianism, and Judaism. They have all received tremendous shocks, and all of them prove by their survival their internal strength. But while Judaism failed to absorb Christianity and was driven out of its place of birth but sect after sect arose in India and seemed to shake the religion of the Vedas to its very foundations. The agnosticism of the Buddhists and the atheism of the Jains all have a place in the Hindu's religion.The Hindu religion alone is the Santana Dharma. About the origin of Hinduism Vivekananda says that Hinduism originated through revelation of the Vedas. The Vedas have no beginning and no end as they accumulated by different persons in different times. The discoverers of these laws (Vedas) were Rishis, and some of them the greatest were women. Just as the law of gravitation existed before its discovery, and would exist if all humanity forgot it, so is it with the laws that govern the spiritual relations between soul and individual spirits. Here it may be said that these laws as laws may be without end, but they must have had a beginning. Thus the Vedas teach us that creation is without beginning or end. And the Vedas are the only scriptures which teach this real absolute God.

Swamiji declares that according to the Vedas 'I' (*soul*) means a spirit living in a body that is nothing but a combination of material substances. The body will die, but the soul shall not die. So the Hindu believes that he is a spirit. The sword cannot pierce him, the fire cannot burn him, the water cannot melt him and the air cannot dry him. The Hindu believes that every soul is a circle whose circumference is no where but whose center is located in the body and that death means the change of the center from holy to body. The soul is not bounded by the conditions of matter. Thus the human soul is eternal and immortal, perfect and infinite, and death means only a change of center from one body to another. The soul will go on evolving up or reverting back from birth to birth and death to death.

The present is determined by our past actions and the future by the present. So there must have been causes to make a man miserable or happy and those were his past actions. That's why some are born happy, some enjoy perfect health with beautiful body, mental vigor, but others are born miserable; some are without hands or feet; others again are idiots, and only drag on a wretched existence. But a man can rid of all these problems by making selfless love with God. As 'Love' is the doctrine of the Vedas so Swamiji asked people to love God for hope of reward in this or the next world, but it will be better to love God for love's sake. A man ought to live in the world but his heart to God and his hands to work.The soul is divine, only held in the bondage of matter but **Mukti**—freedom from death and misery is possible only through the mercy of God who constitutes the religion of the Hindus. But the purity and perfection is the condition for love and attain mercy of God. When a soul becomes perfect and absolute, it must become one with Brahman, and it would only realise the God as the perfection, the reality in its own nature and existence.

Science is nothing but the finding of unity through multiplicity and duality. All science is bound to come to this conclusion in the long run. Manifestation and not creation, is the word of science today; and the Hindu is only glad that what he has been cherishing in his bosom from the latest conclusions of science.

Vivekananda says that God is omnipresent, means to almost the whole world as we think of the extended sky or of space. Hinduism is the world religion as the Hindus have associated the ideas of holiness, purity, truth, omnipresence, and such other ideas with different images and forms. The whole religion of the Hindu is centered in realisation. Man is to become divine by realising the divine. Idols or temples or churches or books are only the support to progress to reach or realise the God. Swamiji says that if a man can realise his divine nature with the help of an image, it would not be a sin. To the Hindu, man is not travelling from error to truth, but from truth to truth, from lower to higher truth. The soul is like an eagle soaring higher and higher, gathering more and more strength till it reaches the Glorious Sun. Thus, to the Hindu, the whole world of religions is only a travelling, a coming up, of different men and women, through various conditions and circumstances, to the same goal. Every religion is only evolving a God out of the material man, and the same God is the inspirer of all of them. First, let us be Gods, and then help others to be Gods. 'Be and make.' Swamiji strictly says that nobody is sinner but everybody is a God. Even if there were a devil, it would be our duty to remember God always, and not the devil. Another important service rendered by Swamiji is to raise his voice in defense of Hinduism[7]. In fact, this was one of the main types of work he did in the West. Christian missionary propaganda had given a wrong understanding of Hinduism and India in Western minds. Swamiji had to face a lot of opposition in his attempts to defend Hinduism.

At the end of the 19th century, India in general, and Hinduism in particular, faced grave challenges from Western materialistic life, the ideas of Western free society, and the proselytising activities of Christians. Vivekananda met these challenges by integrating the best elements of Western culture in Hindu culture. A major contribution of Vivekananda to Hinduism is the rejuvenation and modernisation of monasticism. In this new monastic ideal, followed in the Ramakrishna Order, the ancient principles of renunciation and God realisation are combined with service to God in man. Vivekananda elevated social service to the status of divine service.

According to Vivekananda the people of Northern India are especially grateful to the Southern people, as the great Bhashyakaras, epoch - making Acharyas, Shankara, Ramanuja, and Madhva were born in Southern India. Great Shankara to whom every Advaitavadin in the world owes allegiance; great Ramanuja whose heavenly touch converted the downtrodden pariahs into Alwars; great Madhva whose leadership was recognised even by the followers of the only Northern Prophet whose power has been felt all over the length and breadth of India - Sri Krishna Chaitanya. Vivekananda said that the people of South India are the first and foremost to appreciate and hold on to the message of Bhagavan Sri Ramakrishna. The South had been the repository of Vedic learning, and it is the Shruti still that is the backbone of all the different divisions of the Hindu religion.

Lost in the mazes and divisions of the 'Religion Eternal', by prepossession and prejudice unable to grasp the meaning of the only religion. Whose universal adaptation is the exact shadow of the God it preaches, groping in the dark with a standard of spiritual truth borrowed second hand from nations who never knew anything but rank materialism. The modern young Hindu struggles in vain to understand the religion of his forefathers, and gives up the quest altogether, and becomes a hopeless wreck of an agnostic, or else, unable to vegetate on account of the promptings of his innate religious nature, drinks carelessly of some of those different decoctions of Western materialism with an Eastern flavor, and thus fulfills the prophecy of the Shruti:

—'Fools go staggering to and fro, like blind men led by the blind.' They alone escape whose spiritual nature has been touched and vivified by the life-giving touch of the 'Sadguru'. Well has it been said by Bhagavan Bhashyakara:

—'These three are difficult to obtain in this world, and depend on the mercy of the gods-the human birth, the desire for salvation, and the company of the great-souled ones.

Vivekananda pointed out the system of thought towards which as a center all the ancient and modern Indian thoughts have converged, and the real backbone of Hinduism in all its various manifestations are the Sutras of Vyasa. He says that the Tantrasrepresent the Vedic rituals in a modified form and advisedpeople to read the Tantras in conjunction with the Brahmanas, especially the Adhvaryu portion before reaching into the most absurd conclusions about them. And most of the Mantras, used in the Tantras, will be found taken verbatim from their Brahmans. As to their influence, apart from the Shrauta and Smarta rituals, all the forms of the rituals in vogue from the Himalayas to the Comorin have been taken from the Tantras, and they direct the worship of the Shakta, or Shaiva, or Vaishnava, and all the others alike.

In words of Swamiji, "*throughout the Hindi speaking world, during the reign of Ranjit Singh of the Punjab has made the highest teachings of the Vedantic philosophy available for the very lowest of the low. And I have seen Mehtar Tyagis in the forest of Hrishikesh wearing the garb of the Sannyasin, studying the Vedanta. And many a proud high-class man would be glad to sit at their feet and learn as Supreme knowledge (can be learnt) even from the man of low birth."*[8]

Vivekananda gives a few hints who criticise Hinduism. Very first, people must go to Vedic and Darshanika authorities and begin with the Sutras of Gautama, and read his theories about the Aptas (inspired) in the light of the commentaries of Vatsyayana, and go up to the Mimamsakas with Shabara and other commentators, and find out what they say about the (super sensuous realisation). If we look wewill find a still more lucid discussion into the introduction of Mahidhara to the Yajurvedaas to the Vedas being laws of the inner life of man.

All the sects in India can be grouped roughly as following the Jnana-Marga or the Bhakti-Marga. Both Jnana and Bhakti are everywhere preached to be unconditioned, and as such there is not one authority that lays down the conditions of caste or creed or nationality in attaining Moksha. Vivekananda also instructs people to go through all the Upanishads, and even in the Sanhitas, nowhere find the limited ideas of Moksha, which every other religion has. As to toleration, it is everywhere, even in the Samhita of the Adhvaryu Veda. Society may punish anybody by its disapprobation for breaking any of its regulations, but no man, the lowest Patita (fallen), is ever shut out from Moksha.[9]

Vivekananda says that a Hindu peasant has more religious education than many a gentleman in other countries but he criticised the missionaries who could not understand a line in Sanskrit, criticising the Vedas and all the sacred sources of the Hindu religion. It is not true that Vivekananda was against any religion. He protested against certain methods of missionaries to raise money in America. What is meant by those pictures in the school books for children where the

Hindu mother is painted as throwing her children to the crocodiles in the Gaga? What is meant by the pictures of huge cars crushing over human beings? What have the Hindus done to these disciples of Christ that every Christian child is taught to call the Hindus 'vile', and 'wretches' and the most horrible devils on earth? Part of the Sunday school education for children here consists in teaching them to hate everybody who is not a Christian and the Hindus especially. If a Hindu writes one such line against the Christian religion, the missionaries will cry fire vengeance.

Swamiji says neither Hindus are devils, as the missionaries do not tell the world, nor they are angels, as they claim to be. Swamiji said, *"If foreign friends, you come with genuine sympathy to help and not to destroy, god speed top you. But if by abuses, incessantly hurled against the head of a prostrate race in season and out of season, you mean only the triumphant assertion of the moral superiority of your own nation, if such a comparison be instituted with any mount of justice, the Hindu will be found head and shoulders above all other nations in the world as a moral race."*[10]

According to Swamiji in India religion was never shackled. No man was ever challenged in the selection of his Ishta Devata, or his sect, or his religion. On the other hand, in the West, the field of variation was society, and the constant point was religion. Similarly, Man and Gods show the Hindu religion in the form of their character, their power, and their possibilities of that racial tree which counts culture by centuries, and still stands with the unimpaired vigor of eternal youth. Swamiji appeals to the young people to lay down their comforts, pleasures, names, fame or position to make a bridge of human chains over which millions will cross this ocean of life as no great work can be done without sacrifice. He instructs to bring all the forces of good together and not to care under what banner they march. The results will take care of themselves. Thus India will be raised, not with the power of the flesh, but with the power of the spirit; not with the flag of destruction, but with the flag of peace and love, not by the power of wealth, but by the power of the begging bowl.

References

1. http://hinduism.about.com/od/vivekananda/p/vivekananda. htm, retrieved on 10.12.2012.
2. http://www.belurmath.org/swamivivekananda.htm, retrieved on 10.12. 2012.
3. The Speech by Swami Vivekananda in World's Parliament of Religions, on 11th September 1893 at Chicago, http://hinduism.about.com/od/vivekananda/a/vivekananda_speeches.htm, retrieved on 10/12/2012.
4. http://www.belurmath.org/swamivivekananda.htm, retrieved on 10.12. 2012.
5. *Ibid.*
6. Sharma, Jyotirmaya, 'Cosmic Love and Human Empathy: Swami Vivekananda's Restatement of Religion', Published by Harpercollins. Available athttp://www.outlookindia.com/article.aspx? 283497, retrieved on 12/12/2012.
7. This paper was presented by Swami Vivekananda in Madras. Available on http://www.esamskriti.com/essay-chapters/In-Defence-of-Hinduism-by-Swami-Vivekananda-1.aspx, April 2002, retrieved on 10/12/2012.
8. http://www.esamskriti.com/essay-chapters/In-Defence-of-Hinduism-by-Swami-Vivekananda-1.aspx, April 2002, retrieved on 10/12/2012.
9. *Ibid.*
10. *Ibid.*

will take care of themselves. "This India will be raised, not with the power of the flesh, but with the power of the spirit; not with the flag of destruction, but with the flag of peace and love, not by the power of wealth, but by the power of the begging bowl.

References

[illegible]

Index